Performer as Priest and Prophet

Judith Rock and Cynthia Winton-Henry in their duet, Wrestling with the Angel. *Photo. Kingmond Young*

PERFORMER AS PRIEST and PROPHET

Restoring the Intuitive in Worship Through Music and Dance

Judith Rock
Norman Mealy

1817

Harper & Row, Publishers, San Francisco

Cambridge, Hagerstown, New York, Philadelphia, Washington
London, Mexico City, São Paulo, Singapore, Sydney

Acknowledgments appear on pp. 137–38.

Library of Congress Cataloging-in-Publication Data

Rock, Judith.
   Performer as priest and prophet.

   Bibliography: p.
   1. Music—Religious aspects—Christianity.
   2. Dancing—Religious aspects—Christianity.
   3. Public worship. I. Mealy, Norman. II. Title.
BV178.R63 1988   246'.7   87-46224
ISBN 0-06-066958-6 (pbk.)

88 89 90 91 92 MPC 10 9 8 7 6 5 4 3 2 1

For Meg and Jay

Contents

Preface

In January 1983, Professor Patricia Page, Director of Continuing Education at the Church Divinity School of the Pacific, invited us to teach together at a conference called "The Nonverbal Word of God." This book grew out of that collaboration. we have carried our initial dialogue into the structure of the book by each dealing with his or her artform in response to the five general themes. Each chapter has two voices: the dancer on dance, speaking as choreographer and performer, and the musician on music, speaking as musicologist, liturgist, and teacher. Our separate reflections are then summarized.

In these interchanges, we offer to all interested in the relationship of religion, the arts, and intuitive ways of knowing, some reflections on music and dance as performing arts in the contemporary church: the church struggling toward inclusiveness and a new understanding of *feminine* and *masculine*.

Countless conversations and projects with colleagues and students have shaped and influenced our work. Our heartfelt thanks go to all of those friends and challengers, and also to those who have helped this book along on its journey into the world: Mary Kennan, Bill Wipfler, Larry Hollon, Damian Smyth, and especially our editors at Harper & Row, Jan Johnson and Clayton Carlson.

Judith Rock
Norman Mealy
Berkeley, 1987

Introduction

Lighting the Shadow Side

The impact of the women's movement on the church has set the stage for a new meeting of the church and the arts—a meeting of unprecedented depth and richness. Dr. Norman Mealy and I have written this book to encourage that meeting. The church has, of course, been a patron of the arts at various periods of history, particularly of the visual arts, and particularly at the urging of those in the upper reaches of ecclesiastical hierarchies. This new encounter that our own time offers us includes the performing arts, and promises to affect the lives of women and men at every level of church life.

In recent years, the women's movement has compelled us to see that women and the feminine have historically been forced to occupy the shadow side of the sphere of human experience and understanding: less valued, less well "understood," and perceived as less dependable, less effective, less mature. Christian feminists have shown us the innumerable ways this shadow-side model operates to shape our theology and practice within the churches.

Now, in the late eighties, the church is not only responding to the women's movement with a new willingness to challenge this model of the masculine and feminine as it influences our education and institutions. It is also recognizing that within each of us is a world of masculine/feminine, rational/intuitive, verbal/nonverbal, which is crucial to religious growth and understanding. But no exploration of new territory is easy. Just as women have constituted the shadow side of masculine culture, so has intuitive knowing represented the shadow side of human intelligence: less valued, less well "understood," and perceived as less dependable, less effective, less mature.

As the church embarks on a journey to explore and celebrate the gifts of women and the feminine, it is realizing that part of the work of that journey is the reintegration of our rational and intuitive capacities. The call to reintegrate the rational and intuitive parts of ourselves is coming from all sides. Recent research has shown us the right hemisphere of the brain as the nonverbal and intuitive side and the left hemisphere as the verbal and rational side. But, according to Anne Wilson Schaef, "The newest research suggests that the most functional thinking occurs during the synergistic action of both hemispheres and the brain stem. This union produces especially clear and powerful thinking that is far superior to linear, rational thinking."[1] Half the students in many of America's mainline Protestant seminaries are women, and many denominations are grappling with liturgical renewal and the problems of sexist language and practice. As we turn toward and learn from our collective feminine shadow side, we have an unprecedented opportunity to reclaim the arts as inexhaustible wells of intuition and image, because the arts, in their form and function, depend on and elicit intuitive response.

Intuitive is used to mean many things. In this book, we mean by it ways of perceiving and responding that do not rely on steps taken from the known to the known until enough evidence is gathered to support a conclusion. Intuitive perception and response accept and respect leaps from the known to the *un*known, and build upon unexpected collisions and mergers of unlike with unlike. This book is about the capacity of dance and music, as performing arts in the church, to demonstrate and elicit that kind of knowing. We believe that there are dimensions of the Christian theological enterprise, spiritual journey, and work of worship that can be illumined *only* by the arts calling forth intuitive response.

The five themes we have chosen for the book's chapters take the reader through what seem to us the most important issues, possibilities, and pitfalls of dance and music as performing arts in a church attempting to become inclusive. These five themes are like points on a spiral: the choreographer, composer, performer, watcher, and listener come upon them over and over again as each lives into his or her own complex relationship with these artforms. Against the background of the new feminist presence in the church and the new climate it creates for the church's relationship to the arts, we have asked:

1. What are the elements of music and dance? That is, here is a "music contraption" or a "dance contraption": how does it work?
2. How are dance and music catalysts for theological thinking? What issues do these artforms raise, and what issues can they address?
3. Where do music and dance compositions come from? How do the choreographer and composer create, and what insight into tradition does the activity of the artist offer the church?
4. What role does the artist play in the religious community?
5. How, theoretically and practically, are dance and music vision-bringers for the church?

Those familiar with the literature of dance in the church will notice that what is being urged here is something of an "alternative" point of view with respect to dance in religious settings. Two things in particular stand out. First, dance as professional performing art is stressed, rather than dance as congregational movement or other kind of participatory event. This is because there are several excellent books on congregational movement, but none that focuses exclusively on theatrical dance and its implications for the church. Though some advocates for dance in the church feel that professional theatrical dance creates barriers between people, rather than "building community," I believe that there is a place in the church for dance as performance. (Bach's *St. Matthew Passion* and Handel's *Messiah* do not seem to hinder the creation of community among churchgoers!) One of our hopes for this book is that it can encourage choreographers and dancers who work in religious settings to see themselves as creating the climate for future dance masterpieces, so that the church will possess dance of the same caliber as its best music.

Second, while the relation of the arts, especially dance, to spirituality is often underlined in books on the arts in church, we have tended to underline music and dance in relation to *theology*. The difference between spirituality and theology is notoriously hard to define, and the line between most definitions is as permeable as a membrane. It seems to me that spirituality has to do with practices that help us make a space in our being and life in and through which our response to God is deepened. Theology has to do with formally crafted communications to other people about what God might be like, on the basis of what goes on in that space. By definition, these include communications about human beings in the created world, if we believe that human beings are made in the Creator's image.

Most of what has been written on dance in the church is about how dance helps us make the space—in other words, about spirituality. In this book, the focus is on how both music and dance, as performing arts, *communicate* what we have learned or experienced or perceived in the space. Rather than exploring dance and music as devotional practices, we are concerned here with these arts as formal architectures of meaning: architectures of meaning that communicate through our intuitive rather than through our analytic faculties.

There has been very little serious work done on a theology of dance, though more exploration has been done in that area with respect to music. When dance has been written about theologically, the emphasis has often been on creating an apology for it, because of its unfamiliarity and periodic unacceptability in the church. However, we have tried to consider both dance and music as themselves theological paradigms, rather than being content with "doing theology" about them.

However the line is drawn between theology and spirituality, each always has enormous implications for the other. We hope that those interested in or involved with the arts in the church will be moved to work out the theological implications of this work in a more physically grounded spirituality that embraces masculine and feminine dimensions of being.

Another reason for centering on theology rather than spirituality is that there is always the danger, especially in the Protestant churches, that spirituality will be understood as a private and individual matter rather than as a corporate concern that merits a place on the institutional church's official agenda. Historically, theology seems to stand a somewhat better chance of getting official and corporate attention, and part of this book's agenda is to call dance and music as professional performing arts to the church's official and corporate attention!

The more-than-four-year journey of creating this book has been one of both excitement and sadness. Norm's sudden death in March 1987 ended a joyous process of collaboration. One of the gifts co-authoring the book brought to me was the chance to work with and come to know Norm. Finishing our project is, I hope, in some measure, my gift to him.

Turning around now to look back on this journey of creation, I realize that the book itself is, for me, the result of a much longer journey through the shadow side of my personal experience in relation to the church and to my vocation as a dancer. In 1972, I graduated from seminary as the only woman in my class. During the next years, I tried to make an official and funded place for dance as a liturgical and theological performing art in a mainline Protestant denomination. Simultaneously I tried to create a role for myself within that denomination as an ordained woman and an artist.

I became part of the feminist movement, left it because it seemed to me to value the arts only if they were making a "feminist statement," and have come back to it recognizing that, *because* art is part of our cultural shadow side, it is itself a feminist issue. Like other feminist issues, it raises challenging questions for women and men attempting to create the future in and through contemporary institutions.

Learning about the nature and function of the arts teaches us something about the nature and function of our own intuitive dimension. That is why, when Norm writes as a musicologist about Arnold Schoenberg's *Moses und Aron,* for example, the implications of what he says inform the feminist search for new ways of being and understanding, and help us to see, by implication, why the growing feminist presence in the church creates an exciting new climate for the arts. An oratorio or a dance does not have to make an overtly "feminist statement" with its thematic or emotional content in order to illumine the search for inclusiveness; in its form and function it *is* a feminist statement, because it is an artform communicating intuitively. In the same way, because reflection on the nature of art, its creation, and its function contributes to our understanding of how our intuitive capacities work and what they can do, it also contributes to our efforts to create a more inclusive church and a more inclusive culture.

In 1985, after long self-questioning, I gave up my ordination and joined another denomination as a laywoman. This change to a community that understands itself more in terms of sacrament and less in terms of word has underscored the realization that both sacraments and arts are rooted in a profound appreciation of and attentiveness to the physical world.

Through all these years, I have been working as a dancer and choreographer. Though not without bumps in the road, this has been a joyous and grateful following of a vocation. But it has also created the conviction that the church urgently needs—and is now, I believe, ready—to turn toward intuitive ways of perception and education in order to go on being the historic church in contemporary American culture.

The American churches, along with the other Western Christian churches, have relegated intuitive knowing to the shadow side of human experience partly because of the confusion they have inherited about the relationship of the verbal, the nonverbal, the linear (in which "this" logically follows "that"), and the nonlinear. This confusion is to some extent the result of the church's centuries of reliance on the historically masculine arts of preaching, biblical exegesis, and systematic theology.

Remember the musical *1776?* The enthusiastic and sincere John Adams is forever standing up to make yet another speech about something important. Finally, the long-suffering Continental Congress sings at him in chorus, "For God's sake, John, sit down!" We in the churches, especially in the last four hundred years or so, have often been like poor Adams, forever *talking* about something important. The trouble is not that the main body of our tradition comes to us mostly as words: scripture, hymns, prayers, creeds, sermons, systematic theologies, catechisms. Nor is our problem the fact that words are generally what we have in common to communicate with. The trouble is that, just as we have lost our sense of the relationship of the analytic and the intuitive, we have also lost our sense of how the verbal and the nonverbal work together.

The growing chorus of women and men creating and responding to the leaven of the feminine in the church's life is urging us to recover those relationships—for God's sake! These voices are not telling us to discount or ignore the verbal and the analytic; they are calling us to dive deep into our personal imagery, to watch for our intuitive ways of knowing and to heed them. They are urging us to re-member ourselves as unities of body, mind, and spirit for whom rational language is one gift among many, lighting one path among many.

What happens when the verbal dimension of the church is considered to be the church's most important business? First, this assumption shuts the door on the arts, especially the nonverbal or less verbal arts, and on the gifts they offer us in our search for God and meaning. This assumption also shuts the door on crucial aspects of the women's movement within the church: it devalues the shadow side, the intuitive side, of human experience, and it emphasizes the ascendancy of verbal intelligence over physicality.

In a church whose program is built on the assumption that verbal communication is the most important thing the church does, the arts may be present, even actively supported. But if we look closely at the place they occupy, we will usually find that it is essentially a decorative one. Music fills the space between the verbal parts of worship and is presented extensively only on special occasions or in separate programs for the musically inclined. The Sunday morning sermon is rarely replaced with an oratorio or a fugue. If dance is present, it is more often than not "interpretive," intended to illustrate the verbal content of scripture, prayers, and hymns, as pictures illustrate the pages of a book.

If we look for the roots of our confusion about the

relationship of the verbal and the nonverbal in art and contemporary religion, we find several assumptions about linear and nonlinear communication and perception. First, we tend to call communication that is verbal and linear "sense." Often, the only criterion for deciding that what we are hearing does make sense is that we recognize it as verbal and linear. This assumption is one of the things that can cause us, for example, to treat statements of politicians as communications that make sense, whether they do or not!

Second, we tend to suspect the value of the nonverbal and the nonlinear and call it, if not nonsense, at least less than sensible. This is one reason why the arts are very often regarded, by churches and by our society in general, as frivolous pastimes expendable in budgets, and also why those who make art are rarely perceived by others as doing "real work."

Third, we tend to associate verbal communication with linear structure, and nonverbal communication with nonlinear structure. But we need only consider poetry in relation to the first assumption, and mime in relation to the second, to realize that words can be used in a nonlinear way to create meaning, and that nonverbal expression can depend upon linear communication.

Nonlinear communication and perception function at least partly by condensing experience. The poet is, among other things, a cook who serves us condensed cream of meaning, as Emily Dickinson does in this poem:[2]

Presentiment—is that long Shadow—on the Lawn—
Indicative that suns go down—
The Notice to the startled Grass
That Darkness—is about to pass—

Although there are linear elements in the poem's phrases, its impact depends on leaps of perception from the concept of presentiment, to the idea of sunset, to the whimsical image of "startled Grass"—so that, by the end, "Darkness" is not something we solve by turning on the light. It has become the approaching presence of the night side of human experience.

The poem works because of the way the poet has used *presentiment, shadow, down, startled Grass, Darkness,* and *pass* as points of language around which the listener's or the reader's associations gather. This is one of the ways an artwork creates response.

The silent art of mime, on the other hand, depends on the audience's ability to recognize a linear sequence of events. "Now he is turning into a vampire, now he is opening the window, now he is flying over the city," and so on. The body of the skilled mime—*unlike* that of the dancer—literally "speaks" to us in a linear, nonverbal sequence *that is clearly translatable into a linear, verbal sequence of meaning.* This is why if we want to apply the term *symbolic movement* to any of the body arts, we must apply it to mime rather than to dance.

However, because words are what we usually use in a linear way, we tend to equate the linear with the verbal and the nonlinear with the nonverbal. And because most of us use words more than we use anything else to communicate (or at least we pay more attention to the words in ordinary interactions), we blame them for our liturgical and theological boredom. We say, let's stop using all these words and just *experience* God and art. Or God through art. Or *something* different, something more exciting than three-point sermons and prayers from a book. But what our dissatisfaction is really urging us toward is a deeper understanding of the complementary ways in which both the verbal and the nonverbal lead us into the mystery of the Holy.

Because we have so often done violence to language by identifying it only with our analytic ways of understanding and by using it to explain things away, we need to learn nonverbal ways of communicating and perceiving not only to recover parts of ourselves, but to recover language itself. As the church turns to the arts with renewed interest and contemporary needs, it is important that we not set words and art over against each other, as though one were the villain and the other the savior. We need them both in order to build our theological and liturgical architectures of meaning. Otherwise, we find ourselves struggling to make bricks without straw.

The truth is that words are as physically rooted as arts and sacraments are. All three arise from the glorious, the unaccountable, the creating human body/mind/spirit that is the image of God. All three are for raising questions and for listening to their echoes in the resonant silence of the Holy: all of them are frames for the silence of God as well as for the word of God. They allow us to listen as well as proclaim. As Frederick Buechner said, the business of the church is to point to divine silence as well as revelation. When the prayers are prayed, and the hymns are sung, and the sermon is over, what is left is the mystery and the silence of God.

This is more than a sophisticated way of referring to the repeated human experience of God's absence and apparent unresponsiveness. It is an affirmation of God's presence and action in ways that have nothing to do with linear, analytic, answer-giving verbal logic. There are ideas, insights, and experiences that *only* sound can communicate, others communicated *only* by movement, others that *only* color and line can capture. This is why the arts offer us insight into God, each other, and ourselves that can be offered in no other way. Again, it is important to notice that an artwork does not need to be about relationship or God or feminist theology or liberation theology or evangelism or justice or prayer or the Bible in order to do that. It is enough for it to be an artwork, with an artwork's startling and baffling capacity to be itself, regardless of what we think of it. That is one reason irritation and self-protection often play a part in the response of an audience or a congregation to a new play, dance, musical composition, or piece of visual art. We squirm, slump, frown, raise our eyebrows, sigh. We do our best to maintain some sort of bulwark between ourselves and this new thing that is there before us possessing its soul in confidence. Why? Because no matter who we are or what we have done, we cannot impress a work of art, or intimidate it, or hold it hostage, or make it feel guilty, or strike a bargain with it. All we can do is build a relationship with it. Which makes being in its presence good practice for being in the presence of the Holy.

For many of us, the arts—especially the nonverbal arts—

are less familiar than language, which is one reason they reintroduce us to God's penchant for surprise. Not that the Bible, that deceptively verbal and linear word of God, is not full of the unexpected. It is; but our overfamiliarity with language often keeps us from seeing it. Old Sarah has a baby; the deaconlike Hosea marries a prostitute; Jesus gives wildly enigmatic answers to any given question. But we are not surprised. More often, we are puzzled—even annoyed—and decide that we don't quite understand (or that perhaps the ancients who wrote it all down didn't quite understand). Our trouble is that we insist on assuming that the only business of language is to convey information. The arts, including dance and music, can let us in on the secret that art *and* language, like women and men, have more than one talent: they can make both sense and love.

At the end of the journey of writing a book, one of the things one sees on turning to look back is the books that this book is not, but that need to be written. Though created jointly by a musician and a dancer, this book is not about collaboration between musicians and dancers in religious settings. There are, however, many implications in this present book for such collaboration, and we have hoped that dancers and musicians will come to know more about each other's art—in itself an important prerequisite for working together—from reading it.

Our hope has been that those who read this book will find it a vision-bringer as they work to embody their own visions for the arts in a more inclusive church.

Judith Rock in her Dance of Death. *Photo: Kingmond Young*

Chapter 1

Dance and Music:
Time Arts

TIME ART/BODY ART

Dance is a time art. A dance cannot be framed or preserved in a museum; it lives and breathes for us only in the moment of performance. In its brief incarnation, a successful dance creates a momentary relationship with us by drawing us into the temporal and physical reality that it is and presents. When the dance is over, our world of images and insights has been made larger and more significant, but we are left with nothing tangible: no catchy songs to sing, no lines to quote. The dance cannot even be permanently acquired, like a painting, and hung on the narthex wall.

Although, as a result of the human potential movement, the women's movement, and process theology, we are learning to value relationship and being as well as the accomplishment of tasks, the ephemeral nature of dance can be an initial problem for a congregation. In our culture, we prize the tangible, the product that can be bought or sold, the goal that can be measured and reached in an obvious and public way. But dance has some of the intangible and fleeting character of human relationship. How do we measure a relationship or an insight? What is it worth? How does the ephemeral physicality of a dance become a significant part of the life of a parish? Where does it fit? What are we to make of this rigorous and, to many, unfamiliar artform?

This elusive time-space art whose instrument is the human body has always sparked controversy in the Christian churches. From the beginning there have been those passionately for it and those passionately against it, both as theater art and as liturgical art. The anathemas on dance have received more popular attention, but Christians in favor of dance have also left their mark. Clergy and laity, women and men, these supporters reappear in every age: in religious orders and in Protestant pulpits; in bishops' palaces and on theater stages; in the courts of kings and at the private parties of Puritans; at charismatic meetings and at social justice conferences. They have insisted that the body and the dance are powerful communicators, and that language is not enough when it comes to responding to the mystery of God. In our high-tech century, as we push buttons and watch screens, we need as never before to give our attention to those who remind us of our physical, intuitive, and nonverbal depths.

Because our physicality is rooted in time, one of the tasks of the church is to juxtapose two kinds of time: *kairos* and *chronos*. *Chronos* is the kind of time watches tell, the sequential time we sell as work and count as birthdays. *Kairos* is the other kind of time, known in peak experiences, dreams, meditation, lovemaking, and artistic creation and encounter. *Kairos* is about perception—who we are, who God is, what things mean. *Chronos* is about measurement—how much we have accomplished, how much is left to do. *Kairos* can break in upon, replace, overrule *chronos*. In the Bible, *kairos* is related to the kingdom of God, while *chronos* is the time of ordinary human experience—what the poet W. H. Auden called "the time being."

We go to church and to the theater for some of the same reasons, one of them being that both church and theater can open *kairos* to us and us to *kairos*. The ritual of worship and the magic of the theater are both capable of lifting us out of our usual perceptions and experiences into the larger insight and more significant landscape of this other kind of time.

Dance can communicate in many settings, contributing to this momentary meeting of *kairos* and *chronos*. In the theater,

2

the bursting forth of *kairos* usually depends on a happy conjunction of movement, idea, sound, light, timing, color, costume, personality, and context. For a moment, everything works so that our "willing suspension of disbelief" becomes wholehearted assent. The contrived theatrical image becomes a true image for us, permanently enlarging and illumining our inner world of meaning and understanding. The dancers become heraldic figures, remote from us in the physical space of the theater, emblematic and not personally known. They carry our projections easily and, with the help of these emotional projections, communicate the choreographer's intention to us.

When dance is part of worship, it opens *kairos* to us in different ways, most often without the help of lights, sets, or a large stage space. The dancers in a liturgy are not distant figures in the way dancers in a theater usually are. They are emotionally—and usually physically—closer, sometimes personally known to us, and participants with us in the act of worship. They share the visual space with pulpit furniture, sacred objects, dramatic architecture, and a multitude of other "performers": clergy, musicians, lay readers, ushers, announcement-makers, newly baptized babies, acolytes, and so on. We the congregation are not a silent audience, applauding at the end of the piece, but performers ourselves, with words to say and things to do. The liturgical dancer is a little like the dancer in an opera, a momentary focus in a bewildering array of events. Why add one more character to this more than full cast?

One answer is that we add dance because it is the time art of the human body farthest removed from language. The dancer and the dance are a clearing of silence in the forest of liturgical language. We are reminded that everything comes down, finally, to the human act unadorned by explanation or excuse. Much of worship points us away from ourselves toward our neighbors and God. It is fitting that dance, because its instrument is the silent, muscular body, should point us toward ourselves—our finitude and our choices. "Whom shall I send, and who will go for us?" (Isa. 6:8) is the insistent biblical question. Dancers in the worship service remind us that this question is addressed to us: real people who sweat and pant, soar and fall, who live in specific and complex times and places, struggle with hopes, limitations, and angers.

Contemporary dance in a religious context, whether worship, education, or paraliturgical celebration, helps us encounter and understand theological ideas and also helps us acknowledge and understand our feelings about God and each other. Both as spectacle and as personal action, dance reminds us that everything we know and do, including theology and worship, arises in and is mediated through our bodies. For Christians to deeply experience and understand this obvious but curiously ignored fact is to open the way to a new understanding of Christology, of God mediated through a human body. This perspective also opens the way for a new appreciation of the Jewish Law, of holiness made visible by what is physically done and not done, here and now in the created world.

The Christian idea and event of God mediated through a human body has two dimensions: Christ's incarnation in Jesus, the man of Nazareth; and his birth from Mary, the woman of Nazareth. Because of its physical rootedness in time, dance is a potentially powerful communicator of the earth-rootedness and physicality of Christology. Most often performed by women, dance in the church—when it is well crafted and technically grounded—becomes an arena where women are affirmed as God-bearers: knowers of the Holy and doers of theology.

The repertoire of Body and Soul Dance Company of Berkeley, California, includes a duet for two women called *A Merry Meeting*. This dance is about the visit of Mary, Jesus' mother, to Elizabeth, John the Baptist's mother, when both were pregnant. The costumes for this dance are constructed so that both dancers appear pregnant. We expected the dance to evoke women's experiences of and feelings about childbearing. But we have been surprised and fascinated by the way the dance also enables men to consider their attitudes toward women and women's bodies, and to reflect on their own roles and experiences as male God-bearers.

4

How does a nonverbal artform communicate these theological ideas, or any ideas? We experience a dance as successful, as communicative, when it draws together kinetic excitement, idea, and feeling into a satisfying pattern in time and space. As Doris Humphrey pointed out in *The Art of Making Dances,* we have an innate (though not infallible) sense of design or pattern.[1] We know when an object is physically and visually satisfying to us. Most of us have had the experience of walking into a building and knowing immediately that the space is somehow "wrong," that is seems to reject and disturb the human bodies who are supposed to inhabit it. Or we have idly picked up a pot in a ceramics shop and known, without stopping to analyze how, that this pot is sweet to the hand and "right" for its intended use. This sense of structure and function is part of what it means to be made in the image of the Creator. It may even be that, if we would learn to first consult and then defend these intuitions about structure and function in the face of cost-analysis reports and other practicalities, our sanctuaries, our worship—and perhaps even our theology—would benefit greatly!

Creators of dances weave their patterns to make design in time and design in space. Design in space, which includes where the dancers go in the dancing space, the shapes made by individual bodies, and the spatial relationships of bodies to each other, is the easiest to see. In a worship setting, the architecture and decoration itself also become part of the design in space and should, when possible, be as carefully considered in the choreographer's overall design as the dancers themselves. How can the flood of color from a stained-glass window (and its path through the space as the sun moves), the constricting feeling of a narrow aisle, or the asymmetry created by an off-center cross become effective design elements in a dance?

The color and shape of costumes become especially important parts of the design in space in a liturgical setting. Dancers in cathedrals and in large churches built in the traditional style usually spend at least part of their time in the chancel, relatively far from most of the congregation. Even in smaller settings, visibility can be very poor when the congregation is seated on a single level rather than on an incline as in a theater, and trying to see around pillars, railings, pulpit, and lectern. By their color and shape, costumes can enlarge the dancer's spatial presence and outline the body sharply against the visually "busy" liturgical background. Most important, of course, the costumes underscore and comment on the mood and idea of the dance, enhancing movement, style, and spatial patterns.

A dance's design in time is its overall shape, from beginning to end. Although most watchers do not consciously notice the time design, they experience it as either satisfying or not satisfying. The design in time is achieved by using all of the other elements of choreography, including design in space, floor pattern, movement dynamics, speed, level, rhythmic variation, and sound, to construct a beginning, a climax, and an end that adequately communicate the choreographer's intention or idea. In order to do this, the choreographer chooses key movement phrases, spatial patterns, gestures, and rhythmic patterns, introducing them, building on them, and varying them to create the whole which is a dance. The fact that the music is ending should not be the audience's major clue that the dance is nearly over! By the end, a well-constructed dance has built in the audience a sense that the cup is almost full, that the pattern is almost complete.

Like a liturgy, a dance finds us in one place, and by the end has carried us somewhere else. It does this even though, for performance dance—dance meant to be watched—as for the sermon, we are an outwardly passive audience. When we watch dance, this mysterious journey is accomplished in part by means of kinesthetic identification. If a choreographer has used his or her tools well, the congregation or audience will be physically galvanized, though they appear to be sitting still. They will have a physical sense of identification with the movement taking place before them, feeling the lift and flight of leaps, the spiraling freedom of turns, the sudden change of falls, the surprise of contact when two dancers work together. These physical events and sensations are the heart of dance, and the key to its communicative power.

In order to accomplish its purpose, a dance must reach beyond an audience's visual sense to evoke this kinetic response. It is almost possible to tell from the sound of the applause in a theater when this sense has been collectively awakened in the spectators. The storm of evoked physical energy that flows straight from the center of the body and finds its release in clapping creates a different sound than the intellectual knowledge that an interesting dance is now over. Many congregations do not feel that applause is appropriate in worship, which means that, when a dance done in a worship setting ends, the congregation should have a chance to *do* something: stand and say the creed, sing a hymn, dance themselves.

We can be taken on the physical journey that a dance is, because we have a built-in kinetic sense. When someone stumbles near us on the street, we usually make a sudden move toward that person, reaching out to steady him or her. That sudden move on our part happens because our body has been startled by the other person's stumble into feeling that its *own* balance is lost. We move suddenly—and quite unconsciously—to reassure ourselves that *we* are not falling. The reaching out to help happens after the body has reassured itself, and is the conscious part of our action. Something similar happens to us at the circus. When we watch the tightrope walker or the trapeze artist, our stomach churns, our feet tingle, and we hold our breath. These are physical responses to the fear of falling. But we are not in any danger of falling; we are sitting in the grandstand, looking up. Nevertheless, we are so closely and unconsciously connected to others on a physical level that our bodies identify with those bodies suspended in the air, sometimes to the point of making us acutely uncomfortable.

All dance depends heavily for its communication on this kinetic sense. Once we understand the depth of our physical connection to each other, the charge of inappropriateness that some have made in response to dance as performance in religious settings does not make sense. This charge is sometimes made from the conviction that worship and education should be entirely participatory. But when we understand the kinetic sense, it becomes clear that good performance dance can be

7

exactly that: an exciting experience of participation. Performance by well-trained dancers evokes kinetic involvement in
physical feats beyond the personal ability of most audience
members, so that we are carried out of ourselves and beyond
our physical limitations to new vantage points.

A dance meets us in time and space by means of its idea
as well. If we understand ourselves as a genuine unity of body,
mind, and spirit, we must assume that some ideas, and some
dimensions of ideas, are most easily communicated by means
of the body. Both the arts and religion deal in various truths
about being a human being, and in most religions, some
aspects of these truths have historically been communicated by
dance. The traditionally religious functions of dance are story-
telling and ritual.[2] Today, however, an important function of
dance in relation to Christianity, and perhaps especially in
relation to theologies that lift up women and the poor as
sources of insight into the activity of God, is to r*embody* our
thinking for us. In contemporary culture, there is little to
remind us that thought is as rooted as movement in muscle,
blood, and bone: contemporary dance in religious settings has
the vital task of exploring the nonverbal stratum of ideas.

Although dance can tell a logical story, and is always
constructed by means of a thousand rational decisions on the
part of the choreographer, essentially it draws the viewer away
from conceptualizing through sequential language toward the
more complex levels of our time-space experience. Like dreams,
dance can offer us images of ourselves, the world, and ideas in
which many things are true at once. To enter this nonlinear
world willingly is to relax the control we try to exert over
time and space and to open ourselves to a flood of images and
associations, allowing ourselves to see things in new relationships—and thereby risk new actions and decisions.

For example, in *Abandoned Prayer,* Paul Sanasardo's duet
about Christ in the Garden of Gethsemane, Judas dances behind Jesus, carrying a powerful light, which he turns constantly on the Christ figure. The light streams over the audience,
reminiscent of police interrogations, searchlights, floodlights,
flashlights. Literary images, such as "the light of truth," are

called up for the viewer. The powerful movements of the two men, always in relationship, never at rest, further suggest startling images of evil making good sharply visible, of shadow defining light. During all of these associations, the watcher becomes more and more physically tense as tension builds in the phrases of the duet. By the end of the piece, the viewer is tired, having been involved body, mind, and spirit in the ancient battle and intimate relationship of good and evil.

A choreographer can also use language to enhance the nonlinear, multilevel power of a dance. In *Do You Hear Me, My Little Flower of Paradise?* Margalit Oved recreates her Yemenite Jewish home and family. Speaking, singing, and dancing, she brings a culture to life. melody lines, characters, gestures, and sounds are juxtaposed to create an impressionist presentation of a time, a place, and an intricate web of relationships. Oved uses poetic language, which is the language closest to dance. Speaking of her grandmother's life as "a book," and of her grandmother's influence on her, she says in the dance, "My grandmother wrote a book. Do not look for this book in any library . . . I swallowed it!"

A good dance is a time-space onion: its layers of meaning can be peeled nearly endlessly.

TIME ART/SONIC ART

Music, like dance, is a time art: its sounds occur in time, and no two hearings are the same. The word stems from "Muses," the nine goddess sisters in Greek mythology who nurtured the arts. These feminine Muses had power to call us into greater relatedness with ourselves, others, and God. Euterpe was the goddess of music, and Terpsichore the goddess of dance. Terpsichore is, for many church people, a new acquaintance, while Euterpe is an old, familiar friend. But how well do we really know her?

The musician is one who controls sounds in relation to time in order to create new sonic worlds: worlds made of sound in which we find fresh images and possibilities. Though music can be descriptive like Saint Säens' *Danse Macabre,* or

9

Prokofieff's *Peter and the Wolf,* more often it has, in itself, little or no relation to words and stories. This essentially nonverbal, even nonimagistic reality of music is sometimes not very apparent to us in the church, because we often experience music as hymns or as sound accompanying something happening in the liturgy: people gathering, giving money, or moving from one place to another. The more fully we can open our ears and our minds to the unique gifts music offers us, in relation to nonverbal as well as verbal experience, the richer our relationship with Euterpe—and our worship—will be.

Without time, there is no experience of music, however *music* may be defined. Time and its control lie close to the heart of musical structure and experience. How the crucial element of time is controlled is a measure of the art of music making for both composer and performer, because it is by the ordering of sounds in time that music can communicate to listeners.

The musician's ordering of time allows many "times" to meet. One instance that remains especially vivid for me is the ordination of a young man to the Episcopal priesthood in Berkeley in the 1960s. It was an occasion of joy and solemnity. The ministry of this person was to those who had "dumped" much of their past and who had come to that university city seeking new meaning in the present. Many had gathered together in a community they called "The Free Church," presided over by the new priest. When his wonderfully and colorfully garbed congregation gathered for his ordination, they joined three other communities: upper-middle-class folk of the church in which the service was held, theological students of nearby seminaries, and the mildly cautious clergy of the local diocese.

The resulting congregation's wide diversity was acknowledged in music. The preservice sounds issuing from the loudspeakers set up around the perimeter of the church were those of secular hymnody: Bob Dylan, Joan Baez, Janis Joplin. The entrance of choir, clergy, and bishop was accompanied by a local rock band called "Martha's Laundry." Then, at the midpoint of the procession, the rock sound faded, and another

10

dimension of time came into being—the historical song of the church. The liturgical planners had asked, after a live rock band, what else is there but the unaccompanied human voice? The choir began a "Jesus song," "Alleluia, Sing to Jesus," words written a hundred years earlier and sung to a traditional Welsh melody. The parish church people picked it up at once and the Free Church people joined in—even before they found which book to open! For five glorious verses, six hundred human beings were one body. Time in the present was joined to time past, moving those singers to a remarkable hope for time yet to be.

Time and sound create rhythm, the fundamental organizer of music. Every human being both generates and responds to rhythm. Our heartbeat, which marks our personal journey from past to present to future, has often been considered the basic division of time into regularly recurring units. But our heartbeat varies according to where we are and what we are doing. Similarly, time has rarely been precisely measurable for musicians because decisions about the control of time must be made contextually. A teaspoon is an imprecise measure—and helpfully so. Recipes often carry advice to "correct the seasoning," to use your judgment, for you are the maker! A defined tempo, so many pulses per minute, often needs such "correction" as well. For example, songs sung in a huge, enclosed space by hundreds of people may need to be started more slowly than those same songs sung in a small chapel by a dozen people.

Nonetheless, musicians must measure time. Galileo, toward the end of the sixteenth century, noticed that when any pendulum is set swinging, the time of its swing is directly related to its length. Clocks came into their own, and so did new ways of "keeping time" in music. In many churches, psalm singers were helped by a visible clue to maintain a commonly shared rule of time, a regulated pulse. William Billings of Boston directed all teachers of psalm singing to "make a pendulum of common thread well waxed, and instead of a bullet take a piece of heavy wood turned perfectly round, about the bigness of a pullet's egg, and rub them over, either

11

with chalk, paint or white-wash, so that they may be seen plainly by candle-light."[3]

Early in the nineteenth century, Johann Maelzel of Vienna patented a device both visible and audible, the metronome, still in use today, that measures a predetermined number of clicks each minute. Musicians have their moments of frustration with that impersonal, unyielding click, for while exactness of measure is an important musical goal, it is not the *only* one. Metronomic indicators can themselves be ambiguous, and sometimes need to be changed. Just as a recipe can call for an imprecise "pinch" of salt, the music maker has no choice but to make equally imprecise contextual decisions that alter time.

By ordering *chronos,* music is capable of opening *kairos* to us. This means that music is not only made by ordering time; it also allows us to perceive time as event, which creates the possibility of meaning. Composers make this meaning accessible to us not only by the ordering of *chronos,* but also by making decisions about the "feeling" the music is to embody sonically. For premetronome musicians, the term often used was *mood,* describing the "character" or "spirit" of the music. In Italian, *adagio* means "at ease" ("ad agio") and "slowly," in the sense of "gently" or "peacefully." *Allegro* means "cheerful, good-humored, lively," rather than "fast." Other words indicating quality, not quantity, abound in musical directions: sweet, agitated, brilliant, tender. These premetronome performance directions have a somewhat more intuitive and less analytic quality than the postmetronome ways of dealing with time. In order to make music, and to make music that turns *chronos* into *kairos,* we need to understand and use both pre- and post-metronome ways of ordering time.

No matter what choice we make, the tension between measure and mood is always present. How fast is "cheerful"? How slow is "tender"? The musician who starts a song for others to sing decides. "Cheerful" can become "flip" if a song is too fast; "tender" may become "maudlin" if too slow. The identity of the singing community often dictates these decisions. In charismatic groups, for example, songs are usually bright with a steady beat; in more traditional congregations, songs may be sung with great dignity, thereby providing an anchor to the past. Lutherans are sometimes uneasy with the quick pace of Bach chorales as sung by Episcopalians; in turn, the latter are often dismayed by the rollicking tempo at which songs of personal piety are sung by the more "fundamentalist" churches. The size of the building, its resonance, the quality of its musical instrument, the number of singers, the familiarity of the music—all these affect the musical opening of *kairos:* our perception of and participation in time as meaningful event through the ordering of sound.

Perhaps the most frequently neglected factor in deciding tempo is the *kairos* of the liturgy itself—that is, how music orders and alters perceptions of meaning at different points during the worship service. A song sung at one position in a service may have a different quality from the same song sung at another liturgical moment. "Let All Mortal Flesh Keep Silence," which is in several recent collections of hymns, is a good example. Verbally, this hymn is about putting aside time-bound concerns and turning toward the timeless. This change of focus is suggested by the hymn's first line, calling us to "keep silence," and by its final line, describing the song of the heavenly beings—"Alleluia, Lord most high!"—as "cherubim" and "seraphim" lead the procession of the Christ to the holy place.

When this hymn is sung while money, bread, and wine offerings are gathered and brought to the altar, it is often given a brilliant sound, filling the worship space with the celebratory feeling of the great "Alleluias" in the final stanza and the glory of the Incarnation: "born of Mary . . . the Light of light, descending." The throngs of heaven with ceaseless voice seem to invite us to join them in spirit. Both measure and mood are influenced by this liturgical placement, often one for the "big sound" in churches. But the hymn is also sometimes sung while people receive communion. The quality then is quite different from before; thoughtful reflection and reverence prevail. *Kairos* has changed: the music is likely to be slower and quieter; the singing will probably be meditative rather than acclamatory in quality.

How often we have experienced a vigorous song at the beginning of worship, followed by an awkward moment or two of unplanned silence while the worship leader finds the right place and says something in a timid and tired manner. Or, conversely, how often have we experienced some rather sentimental music played with misunderstood "reverence," only to be followed by a muscular proclamation in a booming voice that suggests a wholly different God.

The pastor of a small church in Wyoming once told me the story of a local organist, who would play inoffensively for about fifteen minutes before the service began. One morning the organist began with the energetic piece intended for later. This cleric, who told me of the sudden charge of energy that went through the congregation, without thinking further leaped up as soon as the music stopped and firmly announced, "Blessed be God: Father, Son, and Holy Spirit!" From there it was a service fully alert. The minister went on to say that previous Sundays should probably have begun: "Blessed be good old God." Music images the Holy by ordering sound in time. It can enable or damage the community's knowledge of the imminent and transcendent God.

In addition to time, music communicates through other elements, including pitch, tessitura, timbre, and their combinations. First, let us look at pitch. *High* and *low* are relational words that center upon context for meaning. What is "high" in one situation is not in another. Often at college football games, for example, people will begin songs at incredibly high pitches and boisterously sing them to the end. In large church conferences the same phenomenon is experienced; hymns are sung quite cheerfully at pitches that would cause much grumbling in the local church on a Sunday morning.

Congregations often find it difficult to imagine singing a particular hymn at a higher pitch than usual and are startled when they discover other communities routinely singing at the higher pitch. *Tessitura,* which has to do with the weaving or proportion of high-pitched sounds within a piece of music, is part of the problem. A song that stays at a fairly high pitch or contains many higher notes can cause discomfort. Our national anthem is a good illustration. "And the rockets' red glare" remains fairly high up—that is, it has high tessitura; many of us drop down an octave to sing it. On the other hand, the familiar hymn "For All the Saints," sung to the music of Ralph Vaughan Williams, seems to bring out the courage of most singers. The final "Alleluia" stays high yet accumulates an energy that is wonderfully expressive of such theological ideas as "holy fellowship" and "communion of saints."

What about *timbre?* Here we mean the quality of sound that distinguishes one instrument from another. Bells, for example, have a different timbre than violins or trumpets, even if they play the same pitch. Voices also have timbre, which creates much of the excitement of choral singing. It is not only pitch, but also timbre, that accounts for the stirring effect of the varying blend of voices in men's, women's, and mixed choruses.

In a Lutheran church in Frankfurt, West Germany, I heard the blind organist, Helmut Walcha, preside over the beginning of a service in a way that movingly demonstrated music's power to create meaning through the ordering of its elements. At this evening service in Advent, he illustrated for his congregation the ability of music to convey the excitement of faith. For a few moments before the service began, the tower bells rang, providing the random mix of rhythms and pitches characteristic of German bells. As the sound of the last bell was fading away, Walcha began a strong organ piece by Bach that lifted one right out of any sentimental journey. He then started the first hymn with a musical introduction that made people not only eager to start singing but also gave them a nonverbal key to the text. The combination of the timbres of the bells, the Bach, and the introduction to the hymn brought us a new understanding of the biblical words "stir up," "awake," "watch." The solemn joy of *maranatha*—"Lord, come"—was present among us.

When music opens the floodgates of response to the Holy, as it did in this Frankfurt church, the power of Euterpe has been recognized and invoked. We begin to know her intimately and to be led by her farther on our journey toward the Holy.

SUMMARY

Both music and dance unfold in terms of time: the time of the clock and time perceived as meaning. When the church invites these performing arts into its midst, a meeting of past and present is created, which in turn creates a context for the future. Each artform is rooted in a particular history; it communicates in the present by making choices in relation to that history, and by following implications of that history into new possibilities. And the gathered community brings, consciously or not, the past tradition of the church and the urgent issues and questions of its own day.

One of the most urgent prophetic voices calling the church to repentance today is that of women. Our need to greet Terpsichore and Euterpe as guides to the intuitive and nonverbal dimensions of ourselves and our experience has never been greater. If we will follow these Muses, these sisters, into the ancient labyrinth of the arts, we will find essential light for the church's new path toward inclusiveness.

An important contemporary meeting place of the arts and the church lies in time perceived as meaning—*kairos*. Chronology becomes meaning when image and experience are born out of quantity and control. Understanding this means gaining access to our intuitive ways of knowing: our ability to see below the surface of things, to hear what has not been said in so many words, to reach beyond what we know in the concrete world of *chronos*. One way to characterize this intuitive knowing is to call it "feminine" in relation to our society's more "masculine" knowing—that is, the more characteristic activities of logic, control, analysis, and concern for quantity and efficiency. This is not at all to say that only women experience this intuitive knowing while only men are concerned for logic, control, and so on. Logic and control are as necessary as receptive waiting and intuitive leaps in the creation of an artwork. But we need to be reminded that each of us has an intuitive, nonverbal, nonlogical repertoire of perceptive abilities that are uniquely tapped, exercised, and increased by the nonverbal or less verbal arts such as dance and music.

The more we understand about the way each of these artforms functions on its own terms, the more possibilities we will be able to see for including the gifts each has to offer us. As the church works at recognizing and being at home in *kairos*, it needs these time arts, because its business is to help human beings find, love, and respond to the Holy. If, as the church has always held, the Holy is beyond all human efforts to fully understand and describe, then we need to use and learn from *all* our ways of knowing and perceiving if we are to get anywhere at all on our spiritual journey.

Judith Rock, Cynthia Winton-Henry, and Phil Porter in their 3-in-1-and-1-in-3. Photo: Kingmond Young

Chapter 2

Music, Dance, and Christian Theology

ISSUES IN MUSIC

We have seen that time arts, like human beings, are always in the process of becoming. This means that they are time-bound. It is in the timeboundness of these arts that much of their significance and possibility for Christian theology lies. From the moment a piece of music begins until it ends, the musician manages a rich interplay of sonic forces. Within that music's time-span, the listener hears many fresh possibilities. But when any given piece of music is over, that particular experience will never be repeated. Music's possibilities are experienced in the present moment; they become fleetingly incarnate in a timebound world. This is true even of recorded music, for we hear each playing of the tape or disk in relation to earlier playings. On the fourth or fifth hearing of the same recording, the listener has already had the pleasure of previous listenings and is more aware of the changing possibilities in the musical experience. It is like reading a Jane Austen novel for the fourth or fifth time. Not only have the earlier readings provided new dimensions, but the reader, too, brings a new set of immediate circumstances to each encounter.

Because sound depends upon the present moment, it reminds religious communities of both stability and change. Music used in weekly services, and repeated several times each year, begins to accumulate its own changing contexts and associations. The impact of such hymns as Martin Luther's "A Mighty Fortress Is Our God," is intensified by repeated use. Each time of singing carries with it memories of earlier singings, often creating for the singer a kaleidoscope of associations with different places, different people, significant events. The associative level of music is very high. A particular combination of sounds often reminds the listener of previous experiences. Many of us readily connect particular pieces of music with important personal memories. In the fact that we do this lies one of the keys to understanding music as nonverbal or partially nonverbal theology.

For example, the associative power of music is one reason why it is so important to work at doing away with sexist language in hymns, whether it be sexist language about human beings or sexist language about the Diety. To sing over and over of men and brothers and their importance to God and the world, while singing little or nothing about women and sisters, is to teach and learn in the name of Christian tradition a clear and, for many, unfortunate message about male and female. Growing numbers of church people feel that such language not only supports injustice, but is also simply inaccurate in our contemporary world. Yet it is difficult for some of us to countenance changing the language of humans precisely because, as they stand, they have such strong links with our personal histories. Changing the language feels like a challenge to treasured memories. However, as we wrestle with this question, we must be aware that hymns, in both their lyrics and music, convey theological messages. When we understand that our response to music is, among other things, an intuitive doing of theology, the issue of sexist versus inclusive language in our hymns becomes one of theological process rather than personal preference.

Music is a profoundly communal art. The composer initiates the experience, the performer brings it into sonic being, and the listener fulfills the process. In the middle of our century, the American composer Roger Sessions wrote sensitively about the way music works in us: "Music is significant to us as human beings principally because it embodies movement of a specifically human type that goes to the roots of our being and takes shape in the inner gestures which embody our deepest and most intimate response."[1] Sessions described a recent performance of a new symphonic work of his as follows:

> The work was beautifully played, and was received with reactions varying from genuine and obvious enthusiasm on the part of a few, to bewildered indifference or even occasional hostility on the part of a majority in the audience. After it was all over, the conductor said to me warmly, "Never forget: the ear is sometimes very slow, the mind is slower, and the heart is sometimes slower still." We composers know that and learn to live with it. But it does not deter us from addressing ourselves with all the resources that we possess to the ear, the mind, and the heart.[2]

The ear, the mind, and the heart of the worshiping congregation need to be awakened to new sounds and thereby opened to new theological considerations. Familiarity must not be the exclusive criterion for the choice of liturgical music. To challenge the listener with new sounds may be ultimately the more nurturing process—and is also called for on biblical grounds. The people in the Bible repeatedly discover that God is nearly always to be found in the unexpected place doing the unexpected thing. The biblical figures whom we revere seem to have encountered the Creator less often in prayer in the temple than in political conflict with kings, or in the working out of complex relationships with other people. They heard God saying to them,

> *I hate and despise your feasts,*
> *I take no pleasure in your solemn festivals, . . .*
> *I reject your oblations. . . .*
> *Let me have no more of the din of your chanting,*
> *no more of your strumming on harps.*
> *But let justice flow like water,*
> *and integrity like an unfailing stream.*
>
> *[Amos 5:21–24, JB]*

In other words, what are we doing first to image and then

21

to create a future in which justice and integrity water the earth?

Music creates the future in worship partly by contributing to the theological growth and insight of the worshipers. Because music is so fully an art dependent upon time, each moment of music in a liturgical context has its own special contribution that takes into account the whole event of worship: participating community, architectural space, biblical themes, physical movement, acoustics of the building, local traditions of the worshiping group, and their communal history.

For congregations, perhaps the most important characteristic of music is its ability to convey meaning. But we sometimes do not realize that the theological communication of hymns is as much a matter of their music as of their lyrics. The lyrics of a hymn sometimes convey one meaning, while the music is proclaiming something else altogether. Our usual assumption is that language is the strongest communicator, the one to which we pay the most attention. But a look at the American Christmas carol, "It Came upon the Midnight Clear" challenges that assumption.

Millions of people in our country love this song's delightful, dancelike melody. Far less familiar to those same millions is the strong double protest of the words. The author, Edmund Sears, was a Unitarian minister leading three small congregations in New England. He was a well-educated parson of great spiritual depth, concerned with the world around him and the people among whom he worked. His poem, which became the words of the hymn, first appeared in the *Christian Register* on December 29, 1849.

Well aware of the poverty within New England's factory towns, Sears tried to help his people make sense of the Incarnation. At the same time, he, like many others in the middle of the nineteenth century, was vigorously opposed to the foreign policy of the United States with respect to Mexico. Many articulate poets and preachers railed against that military adventure, and Sears did his best to interpret God's word for his congregation in the light of his personal opposition.

We have in this hymn, then, a song of double protest:

against poverty and against war. The text begins with a paraphrase of the nativity narrative of Luke:

> It came upon the midnight clear,
> That glorious song of old,
> From angels bending near the earth,
> To touch their harps of gold:
> "Peace on the earth, good will to men,
> From heaven's all-gracious King."

The following stanza speaks of the continuing message of peace, even if we cannot hear it amidst the confusion of life:

> And ever o'er its babel sounds
> The blessed angels sing.

Sears then gets directly to the point:

> Yet with the woes of sin and strife
> The world has suffered long;
> Beneath the heavenly strain have rolled
> Two thousand years of wrong;
> And man, at war with man, hears not
> The tidings which they bring;
> O hush the noise, ye men of strife,
> And hear the angels sing!

Then the minister moves to the theme of poverty:

> O ye, beneath life's crushing load,
> Whose forms are bending low,
> Who toil along the climbing way
> With painful steps and slow,
> Look now! for glad and golden hours
> Come swiftly on the wing;
> O rest beside the weary road
> And hear the angels sing!

We can rejoice that recent hymnals have changed much of the masculine imagery to make the text more useful to all.

23

"Man, at war with man, hears not" often becomes "and warring humankind hears not." But the poet's protest against war is unchanged—and, sadly, mostly unheard!

Why are churchgoers unaware of the serious nature of this hymn text? Why are they unfamiliar with its themes of poverty and war? One reason may be our inability to handle unhappy realities in common song. The book of Psalms is full of wonderful poems of complaint and challenge, written by thoughtful souls so intimately in touch with God that lament and anger were acceptable—even normative—expressions. Largely celebratory on the one hand and penitential on the other, our own hymnody includes relatively few songs whose words and music are written in the spirit of those Psalms. But the more basic reason we do not recognize Sears's hymn for what it is, is that the music, with its bright, cheerful rhythms, conveys a *different* meaning from that of the text, and substitutes that meaning in the mind of the singers. The nonverbal power of music is stronger than the power of the words. That we do not, for the most part, hear or remember "It Came upon the Midnight Clear" as a hymn of protest is a striking testimony both to the power of the nonverbal and the strength of our response to it. How often in our liturgy and education does a response to the nonverbal override a response to the verbal, and how often are we unconscious that this is happening?

Music can alter the meaning of even the most familiar text. Perhaps the most familiar religious text for Christians is the Lord's Prayer:

Our Father in heaven, hallowed be your name, your kingdom come, your will be done, on earth as in heaven. Give us today our daily bread. Forgive us our sins as we forgive those who sin against us. Save us from the time of trial and deliver us from evil. For the kingdom, the power, and the glory are yours, now and forever.

Of what kind of God does the prayer speak? God is both related and apart; God is holy and is cosmic ruler, sustaining and forgiving, saving and delivering. To God belong all power and glory. Knowing both power and mercy, God is present in our lives, yet transcendent in glory. It is this God whom the biblical narrative proclaims. But when this text is set to music, we receive a variety of theological impressions, as the music alters the text's meaning.

Igor Stravinsky gave us two quite different interpretations of the Holy in his treatment of two biblical texts. In an early musical setting of the Lord's Prayer, Stravinsky created a somewhat nostalgic recollection of the church in Russia. The music suggested a God who was dimly mysterious and modestly withdrawn from social action. But later, in *Abraham and Isaac,* the same composer, now in his eightieth year, gave us a very different picture of an actively present God who demands obedience and who blesses those who listen to God's word and obey it. The intensely serious music with which he surrounded this biblical story tells us that Stravinsky had come to a new understanding of God's power and glory. For him, and therefore for us listeners, these pieces of music convey two widely differing images of God, sonic images so different that each might be considered a small "theology" in itself.

In Mozart's opera *Don Giovanni,* music becomes a striking conveyer of theology. The composer communicates to us a God who offers a terrifying choice: repent or be damned. Mozart's musical definition of the Don himself opens a window onto the emptiness of a godless life. Don Giovanni to Mozart is a nobody, a nothing. In every aria but one, the Don's music is derivative: it takes its character not from some inner integrity or strength, but rather from the person with whom the Don is double-dealing. The one exception is the famous drinking song in which the music describes an inane human being. Short musical phrases of two measures each are repeated over and over, with no change in harmonic or rhythmic detail. By the time we have heard this silly tune twenty times, we are well aware of the biting truth of Mozart's description of the person inside the Don: no one, a void, a person emptied of all that makes human relationships have meaning. The terrifying choice? Repent or be damned.

Composers of theatrical masterpieces and religious performance pieces, and composers of familiar hymns, offer diverse images of God out of their complex variety of experience—experience that is, by its nature, ambiguous. That is, human beings glimpse reality from one perspective at this moment, and from another perspective at another moment. Because we are timebound, we can never see reality in its wholeness. The church possesses innumerable pieces of music that embody glimpses of the Holy. We hear sonic images of God the Holy Other in rich medieval melodies; God the great sustainer in seventeenth-century Scottish Psalm tunes of immense dignity; God the loving forgiver and friend in the gospel songs that, a century ago, helped thousands to find a spiritual anchor in the strange and lonely cities of England and the United States.

The church also possesses, of course, an endless treasury of wordless music, including many of the world's musical masterpieces. But if we visit a variety of churches, and listen to the organ and other pieces chosen for worship, we might conclude that we worship a God who is peaceful, sweet, uncontroversial, and amiably to be ignored. Once in a while, we find a community at worship listening to music suggesting strength, clarity, and thought. Occasionally—but far too seldom—a Mozart string quartet or a Hindemith sonata for piano and flute greets our ears upon arrival at church.

The church of St. Severin on the Left Bank in Paris is one place where the theological dimension of music is routinely recognized. This five-hundred-year-old church still ministers to the thousands who live around it: poor people, shopkeepers, and the university students and professors who have made the Left Bank such a remarkable area. There in that crowded Gothic building, the word is proclaimed and the liturgy comes alive each Sunday morning, partly because the congregation has learned to reflect on the word through the nonlinear, nonverbal power of music. After one reading from the Bible, there is silence, time for the community to think about what they have heard. After a second reading, there is more silence, and then the sermon: brief and clear. When that is over, the preacher sits down like everyone else, and music suddenly bursts forth from the rear gallery. For the next few minutes, a musician improvises upon the word of God. Improvisation?

And *proclamation,* which does nonverbally what few words could do for this diverse congregation.

Johann Sebastian Bach spent a large part of his life in the Lutheran community at Leipzig, speaking musically from faith to faith. In 1727, Bach first performed his musical setting of the Passion narrative as we find it in Matthew's Gospel. Completed for a Good Friday service at St. Thomas's church, Bach's *St. Matthew Passion* may be one of the most profound theological commentaries of the eighteenth century. His understanding of human sin and the forgiveness of God is constantly shown forth. One illustration of Bach's grasp of the meaning of health, salvation, and the costliness of life is a set of two musical portions adjacent to each other. The Passion narrative has just concluded its description of the placing of Jesus on the cross:

So also the chief priests, with the scribes and elders, mocked him, saying, "He saved others; he cannot save himself. He is the King of Israel; let him come down now from the cross, and we will believe in him. He trusts in God; let God deliver him now, if he desires him; for he said, 'I am the son of God.' " And the robbers who were crucified with him also reviled him in the same way. [Matt. 27:41–44]

Bach now comments upon the action. A dreadful scene is set by a quiet, fragile string sound pressed down by the edgy, reedy sound of oboes in turmoil turning around a central pitch. Over it all is the high, tense cry from a solo alto voice, "Ach, Golgotha, unselges Golgotha!" The "wretched" place of the crucified Jesus is given a remarkably tragic sound. Right after it, Bach, using the same group of instruments in quite different ways, shows us Christ the King on that cross offering his love and inviting us to follow. The same solo alto voice bids us to "see Jesus there with his hands outstretched." All of the twisted, turgid dissonance of the first part is gone, and in its place is a bright and joyous serenity: the serenity of love in obedience, or love offered as amazing gift.

Yet another illustration of music's ability to sharpen our insight into a known text is Bach's tremendous chorus directly after Judas's betrayal kiss.

27

Now the betrayer had given them a sign, saying, "The one I shall kiss is the man; seize him." And he came up to Jesus at once and said, "Hail, Master!" And he kissed him. Jesus said to him, "Friend, why are you here?" Then they came up and laid hands on Jesus and seized him. [Matt. 26:48–50]

What happens next is incredible. With the simplest of musical means, Bach begins an aria that is quite literally unearthly: the usual ground bass of Baroque music is removed. Two soloists, an alto and a soprano, sing a lyrical line of quiet beauty: "So is now my Jesus captured." In the midst of that ethereal sound, one chorus breaks in with a loud cry, "Free him! Stop that! Don't bind him!" The fragile sound continues as though the chorus had said nothing. Now the soloists speak about the light of the moon and the sun dimming because "my Jesus is captured." The chorus interrupts once more with a fierce shout, and the soloists continue their quiet comment: "They lead him away; he is bound." There is a wondrous quality of holy otherness about the sound, as though what is happening is beyond our ability to comprehend; we can only marvel at the cosmic significance of this story.

Both choruses and both orchestras interrupt in rage. "Are lightning and thunder lost in the heavens?" Then, with a startling harmonic shift, the voices call upon the fires of hell to do something about this betrayal. Immediately, the biblical narrative resumes with an act of violence: one of those with Jesus strikes out against a servant of the High Priest and cuts off his ear. Jesus quickly rebukes his followers:

All who take the sword will perish by the sword. Do you think that I cannot appeal to my Father, and he will at once send me more than twelve legions of angels? But how then should the scriptures be fulfilled, that it must be so? [Matt. 26:52–54]

Fulfillment of divine purpose rises above human protest. The serenity of the soloists is in enormous contrast to the wild anger of the full ensemble. It is the peace of God that passes understanding; and it is the music, far more than the text, that underscores the dichotomy between the ways of God and the ways of humankind.

All of this is theology through music, a gift for those who will listen with open ears and open mind. This gift is given through a lively interplay of intelligence and feeling. it acknowledges both the depth and the limitations of our human perceptions of reality. Music's ability to be theology underscores the importance and strength of the intuitive and the nonverbal in shaping our understanding of God; the musician is a crucial contributor to the never-finished theological growth of the church.

ISSUES IN DANCE

The seventy-sixth Psalm tells us that "God's tent is pitched in Salem, God's home is in Zion" (Ps. 76:2, adapted). For those who hold biblical faiths, God is intimately present and actively involved in the created world and the lives of human beings. Gregory Thaumaturgous, a third-century Christian missionary, echoed this sense of God in the world: "Dance with me, Jordan River, and leap with me, and set your waves in rhythm, for your Maker has come to you in body!"[3] Dance that stands within the Jewish and Christian traditions is dance rich in detail, surprise, and relationship, dance engaged with the human world of time and space, and therefore with contemporary issues: personal, political, theological.

Because dance communicates kinetically, muscle to muscle and bone to bone, it has a way of ducking under our intellectual and rational guard to surprise us with deep and unexpected feelings. It is the human act, unadorned by excuse or explanation, that freezes our blood, strengthens our resolve, moves heaven and earth. An official in occupied France signs his name to a document, and thousands of Jews die. Gandhi lies fasting on his bed, and peace returns to India. Jesus is nailed to a cross, and the tombs of our hearts are opened. In a more limited and temporary way, dancers in the magic space of performance, which can include the chancel and the social hall as well as the stage, are able to focus for us our longings

29

and absurdities, our temptations and allegiances. Dance does this by confronting us with the here and now of things; this sense of here and now is the artform's most important link to the spirit of the biblical narrative.

If the biblical record is taken as a reflection of human experiences of God, we can find in it two perceptions of who God is and what God does in the world, both of which suggest directions for the arts in the church. The first is the most obvious: God the creator, maker of inexhaustible diversity and beauty. The second is God the questioner, challenging us, surprising us, calling us beyond complacency. Responding to God the creator means making and delighting in beauty, means play and a profound respect for the aesthetic dimension of human experience. Responding to God the questioner means realizing that the arts are equally meant for depeening our response to injustice, and for grappling with the fact that, as one wise pastor put it, "Life is very terrible."

When the disciples of John the Baptist asked Jesus if he was the Christ, his answer was characteristically concrete and focused on this world: "Go back and tell John what you hear and see; the blind see again, and the lame walk, lepers are cleansed, and the deaf hear, and the dead are raised to life and the Good News is proclaimed to the poor" (Matt. 11:4–5, JB). In other words, we are to look for God in the midst of our human and worldly decisions, relationships, and struggles. This suggests that the purpose of the arts in a religious context is to help us live with courage and open eyes in a world where we can be sure God will meet us not only in prayer and worship, but in the faces of the poor, in our lonely decisions at three o'clock in the morning, in the glory of the creation, and in our intimacy with those we love. The poor, our decisions, our delights, our loves, and our hates are among the things choreographers in religious settings need to be making dances about.

We are creatures whose Creator has chosen to dwell with us, to come to us through the world of created things, which also means coming to us through our bodies. All our knowledge, including our knowledge of God, comes to us through the body/mind/spirit totality that we are: through our senses, our thoughts, and our feelings. Biblically rooted dance affirms our body/mind/spirit construction, and challenges us to do three things: to meet God in the midst of the world, to break the idols we make for ourselves, and to shake ourselves out of a complacent attitude toward the misfortunes of others. This kind of dance raises questions and responds to issues. Its implicit assumption is that nothing is sacred except God. However, when we approach dance in this way, we need to ask at least three questions. First, is dance that embodies issues propaganda? Second, what is the role of humor in the performing arts of a religious community? And third, can we talk meaningfully about "sacred" dance?

Dance that embodies issues is dance that "moves" us to image the future. When art helps us image the future, it momentarily frees us from the enchantment of the way things are now so that we can experience, for a moment, what might be possible. Dances that offer us these moments of vision do so in a variety of ways. A few dances are shimmering glimpses of a sort of New Jerusalem, in which humanity seems either unfallen or finally transformed. *Esplanade,* by Paul Taylor, is such a dance. Its entire joyousness, lack of pretense, and endless physical splendor are my own favorite glimpse of what it might be like to live in the kingdom. Not that Taylor set out to make an eschatological dance; as far as I know, he did not. But in *Esplanade* he has created a world so luminous that it lights up more than itself.

Other dances image the future by recreating a world from the past and allowing us to reexperience, or experience for the first time, the grief of its loss. These dances help us create the future because their implied question is, "Shall this happen again in some new way? Or have we repented, have we learned?" A solo piece in the repertoire of the Crowsfeet Dance Collective, *Trail of Tears,* by Pamela Gray, tells us, with dancing, speaking, and hand signs, about the defeat of the American Indians. With dignity and sorrow, but without stridence or sentimentality, the dancer evokes the battles and retreats of the tribes as she retreats across the stage. By the end of the piece,

31

however, we are not so much sorry for them as ashamed of ourselves and wishing not to inflict the same suffering again.

In a similar way, a dance can invite us to image the future by focusing our attention on a contemporary situation so that we experience it kinetically and are left asking ourselves how we are involved and how we can respond. Cynthia Winton-Henry's dance about violence, called *Rachel Weeping,* does this by presenting the problem of American family violence in the context of Hitler's Holocaust and the present strife in Central America. Without pushing us to adopt a particular "party line" or course of action, the choreographer implies in the structure of the dance that we will continue to destroy others at home as long as we persist in destroying those who disagree with us abroad, and that all violence is family violence. Because both the Central American section and the family section of the dance are seen against the background of the Holocaust, that highly rationalized orgy of destruction, Winton-Henry effectively takes away any possibility we might have had for rationalizing our own violence.

Because they affirm and draw on nonrational, intuitive imagery, the arts allow the church to move beyond "strategies" and "task forces" in choosing and creating a future. Partly in response to the women's movement and the flowering of women's gifts within the church, both women and men are turning toward a more process-centered and less task-oriented organizational style. We are becoming less concerned with answers and hierarchies, and more concerned with questions that make space for new choices. The level of the self from which artistic imagery comes offers us complex images of wholeness that will, if we allow ourselves the time and space to live with them, deepen the wisdom of our organizational decisions. Because women must live with constantly changing bodies, we know, without thinking about it, that change, development, and new life are the result not only of decision and action, but of waiting, contemplating, and living with events. This kind of attentive "waiting with" is part of what the artist does in the creation of a work, and part of what the audience does in response to it.

The art we live with in this way reappears in the daily

patterns of the future. Which means, of course, that we have to ask what kind of future we want. If part of our contemporary task is to bring forth a newly inclusive church that embodies the insights, repentances, and commitments of contemporary women and men, what do we need to be imaging in our art? The traditional male-ordered and rationally oriented church? A feminist church conceptualizing itself only in images of birth and the female body? A Jungian church in which the Anima and the Animus preside together at the altar? Or something else not yet dreamed of? Whatever our vision of the future may be, we will get there only if we can make room for and respond to the new, the strange, the unexpected imagery created by the artists in our midst.

The difference between propaganda and dance that deals with issues and ideas in terms of complex and non-solution-oriented imagery is that propaganda urges *one* party-line solution to a particular problem. We will avoid making or supporting dance that is propaganda if we remember that God seems to leave each one of us free to respond or not to God's call and presence. Biblically authentic art can do no less. We are urged to "choose life," but never forced. Dance that raises questions and addresses issues is at its best when it is open-ended. Of course, opinions vary greatly about where open-endedness ends and lack of commitment begins! Recently, Body and Soul was asked to submit a videotape of a dance, as part of the selection process for companies to be included in a social justice dance concert in San Francisco. We sent a tape of *Basic Training,* by Phil Porter, which we have always considered a provocative statement about the dangers of American militarism. But the tape was returned to us with the explanation that the piece seemed too open-ended.

Open-endedness, then, is to some extent contextual. Nevertheless, neat and simplistic moral and theological solutions, unmistakable and unchanging "white hats" and "black hats," ring false with people who have dared to look closely at themselves and others. Even Jesus was moved to say, when someone called him "good teacher" and asked him for a quick answer to the question of salvation, "Why do you call me good? No one is good but God alone" (Mark 10:18–19).

What issues might dance address in a religious context? One way to answer this question is to continue the list (by no means exhaustive) of some of the issue-oriented dances I have experienced as audience member, choreographer, or dancer in both church and theater. This list includes Kurt Joos's classic antiwar dance, *The Green Table,* created in Germany in the 1930s; Richard Clairmont's spoof on superficial piety, *True Confessions*; John McConville's *Take-Off,* about the hilarious risks of getting to know oneself and the opposite sex; Body and Soul Dance Company's *3-in-1-and-1-in-3,* about finding one's way through the maze of theological language; and Carla De Sola's *From the Diary of Anne Frank,* a poignant meditation on the human spirit in the midst of war. These dances confront us with questions: What is morality? Can evil bring about good? When is it appropriate to defy a government? Why is there so much suffering? What is masculine and what is feminine? How and what can post-Holocaust believers believe?

The challenge of some of these dances— *True Confessions, Take-Off,* and *3-in-1*—lies in their humor. They invite us to break our idols by making us laugh at things about which we are usually quite serious, such as piety, sexuality, and theology. To laugh at something is not necessarily to discount it; to laugh may be the beginning of appreciation, of moving toward a thing with new freedom. G. K. Chesterton commented perceptively on our human penchant for seriousness, and for taking our seriousness so seriously:

We are perhaps permitted tragedy as a sort of merciful comedy: because the frantic energy of divine things would knock us down like a drunken farce. We can take our own tears more lightly than we could take the tremendous levity of the angels. So we sit perhaps in a starry chamber of silence, while the laugher of the heavens is too loud for us to hear.[4]

A certain kind of seriousness is a pitfall when we deal with an artform in a religious context. It arises from several sources: confusing the artform itself with what motivates the artist, insecurity about technical and choreographic skills, and secret uncertainty about the appropriateness of art in church. These confusions and uncertainties account for the unfortunate self-importance of some dance made for religious settings. It is time for us to admit that the ludicrous stiffness and—dare I say it?—self-absorbed earnestness of this kind of "religious" dance is not only highly questionable theologically; it is downright off-putting to those who watch. We may respond that we are not dancing for the watcher, we are dancing for God. But is that really what we are doing? Surely we do not believe that God needs our dance. We may be helped out of this confusion by remembering that even the Benedictines, those unsurpassed singers of Gregorian chant, emphatically state that they do not chant "for God"; they do not chant because God somehow needs their chant. To be sure, they chant "to the glory of God." But they are quite clear that it is *they*—the community—not God, who need the healing, soaring, timeless beauty of the chant. In the same way, it is our communities that need the communication our dancing has to offer. When dance is made to be watched, its primary flow of communication is outward toward real people, people like us.

What I am trying to say is astringently summed up in the comment of a clergyperson about dance he had recently seen in a cathedral liturgy. Very perceptive about the arts in the church, and also aware of his own physical reserve, he expressed his disappointment with what he had seen by remarking, "It was so tight and solemn! I could have choreographed it myself."

Dance like this is sometimes made in the name of "sacred" dance. But is that really a helpful term? When the acts of making dance and dancing in a religious context are confused with the power of the Holy, about which a dance merely attempts to communicate something, we are in danger of thinking that the dance itself is somehow sacred. To call one segment of an artform "sacred" implies that the rest of that form is unacceptably "secular" and suspect. If we insist on this division, we weaken the artform in a religious setting, because when only certain elements and styles are acceptable, expression and creation become limited to only those elements

35

and styles. Making anything means making choices: the choreographer must be courageous and knowledgeable enough to choose, from his or her understanding of dance history, technique, and style, the elements needed by a particular dance—no matter how surprising those elements might at first seem!

A longer look at the place and use of ambiguity as a communicative element in the arts can help to clear up our confusion about what is sacred and what is not. One of the meanings of *ambiguity* is "being on the boundary line" between two things. It is the state of being neither wholly in the light nor wholly in the darkness, of being in a morally and theologically dappled place. The boundary line, this place of shifting light, lies between all dualities: good and evil, human and divine, flesh and spirit, male and female, life and death. The use of ambiguity in the arts, and in theology, is partly the active resistance of the temptation to herd God and human beings onto the side of this border marked "good," "divine," "spirit," and "life." Because as soon as we give in to that temptation, the only thing left is to build a wall to keep out "evil," "human," "flesh," and "death." We can also understand the sexist practices of the church and the culture in terms of this image of wall-building: "male" has been most often included in the compound along with "good," "divine," "spirit," and "life," while "female" has been relegated to the other side.

Choreographers working in religious settings sometimes misunderstand their task and give in to the sheep-dogging and wall-building temptation, with the result that their art moves from "the boundary line between" squarely into the province of "good," "light," and so on. The trouble with this artistic and theological decision is that *all* human undertakings and categories, including the good and the moral, are, by their nature, ambiguous: made up of contradictory experiences and realities. Psychologists since Freud have been warning us that our conscious desires and insights are not the whole story, and theologians repeatedly remind us that the only *unambiguous* reality is God.

We live in the midst of ambiguity because we continually experience not only beauty, goodness, and truth, but also personal limitation, timeboundness, and estrangement. Each of us sees the world from within the restrictions of a limited personal existence. In an encounter with an artwork, we are sometimes enabled to transcend our personal and restricted view of things and see, momentarily, a panorama of meaning. When this moment occurs, what the artist has done is focus our human (by definition, ambiguous) situation so clearly and in such detail that we see beyond it; we become sharply aware of the *un*ambiguous reality for which we hunger. It is as though a momentary lull lets us hear the approaching footsteps of whoever or whatever we long for.

Ambiguity as a communicative element in dance means seeing and communicating such things as goodness and hope and also such things as estrangement and failure. It means communicating the presence of God, the absence of God, and also the threat of God, because these are experiences that coexist in all human efforts and institutions, including religion and dance.

Several years ago, I made a solo dance called *Baptism,* which forced me to think about the communicative aspect of ambiguity.* *Baptism* is about the contrast between the ordinary Sunday morning church service and the realm of mystery and power toward which the service and its sacraments, including baptism, point. The dance begins with the dancer seated on a chair center stage, wearing a straw hat with a ribbon and an ivory colored dress, and holding a hymnal and the kind of cardboard fan once found in southern churches. The dancer becomes increasingly inattentive to the worship service; she fans herself, leafs through the hymnbook, yawns, and finally dozes. The lighting, which has been rather gray and indoor, becomes a sunny yellow, and the sound of waves breaking begins to be heard. With a sudden sense of freedom and enlarged space, the dancer finds herself on a beach. Her movement

---

*Here and elsewhere, I use my own work as an illustration because I can write about it from inside and out, as choreographer, dancer, and, sometimes, observer.

begins to suggest release and delight in the change of scene as she takes off her hat, lets down her hair, basks in the sun, and dances at the water's edge. Her movement becomes more and more sensuous as she swims, dives, and lets the water rock her and take her where it will. Then she realizes that the tide is coming in, and her pleasure becomes fear that she will be drowned. She gathers her scattered belongings from the sand and takes refuge on the chair. The dance ends with the dancer standing on the chair, clutching hymnal, hat, and fan and looking anxiously out to sea as the tide comes in around her.

Audiences are apparently very drawn into the opening and middle sections of the dance, identifying with the dancer and kinetically experiencing release and abandon in the shedding of hat, fan, and hymnbook, and in the water-related movement. Many comments after performance, however, indicate that the change in feeling tone to fear and dread, the anxious gathering up of the abandoned objects, and the retreat to the chair are very disturbing. The usual question is, "But why should she be afraid? What is frightening about baptism, or about Jesus?"

Part of this response to the end of the piece points to a recognition of the ambiguity the dance communicates. Baptism is a sacrament of the church, an event Christians usually place on the "desirable" side of the desirable/undesirable duality. Part of the ambiguity of the dance consists in moving the concept of baptism out of the space marked "desirable" onto the boundary line between desirable/undesirable. The dance begins with an ambiguity for which most everyone in the audience would be prepared. Many churchgoers have at some time been bored in church, and most nonchurchgoers would not be surprised to learn that church is occasionally boring. But by means of that rather superficial ambiguity, the audience is drawn on to confront another ambiguity for which they may not be prepared. It can be called the fear of the very good. Or, biblically, the feeling Isaiah is having when he responds, on seeing God, "Woe is me!" What if the good turns out to be terrifying? It is at that point that the dance becomes disquieting. What is intended to flame into meaning at the end of this piece is that the tapwater in the baptismal font is an inlet of the sea of God, perfectly capable of sweeping us, our expectations, and our categories away.

The above is, of course, the choreographer/performer's description of what happened in the dance and in the audience. It does not deal with another level of ambiguity present in the time arts. That is, it does not deal with the structural flaws of the piece, with the dancer's failures in performance, or with various "technical" problems, such as the fan once breaking at the beginning of the dance. This level of ambiguity is a crucial difference between a performing and a nonperforming art. No matter how many times a novel is read, or a painting is contemplated, the words on the paper and the paint on the canvas do not, of themselves, change. But because of its greater time-boundness, a dance, like a piece of music, is never the same dance twice. Dance automatically includes a layer of ambiguity in relation to issues of time and human failure that less time-bound forms do not possess.

This built-in layer of ambiguity makes the time arts especially potent catalysts for theological reflection. God may not change, but we do, and therefore our theology-making must focus on that reality as well as on God's changelessness if theology is to have any impact on our lives. Ambiguity helps us to identify strongly with characters, situations, and images; in their complexity, we recognize ourselves, though often reluctantly. The choreographer who communicates in this way evokes in us, out of a deep sense of the entanglement of good with evil, joy with sorrow, and fear with longing, an acknowledgment of those same entanglements in our own lives and a new realization that we will find joy and understanding in those labyrinths or nowhere.

It is especially important that people who understand themselves in terms of biblical faiths should wrestle with this complexity. No mature religious faith is a simple matter in which one act or decision means only one thing or brings about only one result. When the people in the Bible ask direct questions about meaning, they generally do not get simple, one-dimensional answers. "If you have faith as a grain of mustard seed, you will say to that mountain, 'Move hence to yonder place,' and it will move" (Matt. 17:20); give "to Caesar the things that are Caesar's, and to God the things that are God's" (Matt. 22:21). Simplicity is not the key to the people and the narrative of the Bible, just as it is not the key to us and our lives. If dance, or any art, is to be a valid part of religion, it must acknowledge, participate in, and illumine human complexity. Illumining our humanity means making it visible and accessible, not simple.

It may be that our wistful suspicion that religion, art, and we ourselves are really simple—if only we could find the key to understanding—is in part the result of too much emphasis on rational thinking. In logic, every proposition is true or false, and leads to one correct conclusion. As I was taught in my college logic course, "Everything is either a cabbage or not a cabbage." But in our lives, every choice, feeling, and action has a dozen ramifications and leads to a hundred possibilities. We must and do make judgments about good and evil. But if we are biblically grounded, we do so remembering God's "answer" to Job, which is not an answer at all, but another question: "Were you there when I made the world?" Dance as an artform in a religious community ought to remind us that both art and faith ask complex questions and elicit complex responses.

This sort of complexity in dance has nothing whatever to do with vague intentions on the choreographer's part, with lack of precision in handling the elements of dance, or with the desire to mystify the audience. All successful artistic communication, even of ambiguity, depends on clarity, skill, and the genuine desire to communicate. The skillful choreographer is able to focus the specific, the individual, the passing event against the backdrop of the question of meaning. When that is done, we are given the gift of seeing ourselves framed and lit so that, for once, we get a good look at the creature. Somehow the performing space is an even better place than the bathroom mirror for finding out the truth about ourselves.

The vision given, if it is a true and powerful vision, raises of course the question of evil. To say that ambiguity is an important element of communication in dance is to say that a good dance can show us evil, both in ourselves and in the world around us. Too often the religious artist, including the choreographer, has tried, like a frontier sheriff, to pick off the bad guy with a six-shooter as the good guy and bad guy grapple with each other in the dust. In popular Christian art in recent years, and perhaps in dance in particular, the besetting theological heresy has been the Manichaean one, the idea that light/good and dark/evil were originally separate and will be again. For the Manichaean, there is nothing to be learned on the border between dualities; the only valuable thing is to get good and evil clearly separated and to slip into the stockade of light before the gates are closed. This worldview weakens human beings as makers of moral choices, because it refuses to recognize the closely woven pattern of light and shadow in our lives. This Manichaean attitude can also cause the religious artist to be discounted in the secular world, if he or she is perceived as a facile builder of walls between good and evil and between the saved and the unsaved.

David Bailey Harned said in his book *The Ambiguity of Religion* that a Manichaean separation of good and evil implies the separation of truth and the physical world. But the physical world is the realm of all art, of all incarnate vision. Therefore, the would-be artist tending toward a Manichaean theological position may not take the trouble to do justice to the technical requirements of his or her artform, because he or she may not cherish the physical world enough to bother. This Manichaean attitude is echoed in the words of those who assert that they want to dance in the church, dance while others watch, but that they have no need of technical skill, because their dance is "in the spirit" or "from the heart" or because "God has given them the gift of dance." The sobering incarnational truth is that the gift of dance is given through the body: most often through long years of pliés, relevés, and sweat.

The question of evil is an important one in the encounter of religious people with art. There is sometimes a strong negative reaction to artworks that communicate the inextricable mixture of good and evil in human life. One group of adults in a city parish refused to read *Zorba the Greek* in a seminar on theological issues in modern novels; they considered Zorba a "dirty old man" and were offended at being asked to make his acquaintance in a church study group. A seminary student, assigned another contemporary novel, lamented that if only she could have known its characters *before* they became in so many ways unlovable and damaged, maybe she could have loved them.

The surprising and biblical point of art that presents the ambiguity of our human situation in all its confusion, poignancy, and unsavoriness is that in no other way can the biblically rooted artist be faithful to the record of God's will and presence as we have received it in the Bible and in our historical religious traditions. This becomes especially evident when we consider the Christian doctrine of the Incarnation, the belief that in Jesus, God's Word became flesh and dwelt among us. If ambiguity is the essence of our human situation, what the Word became flesh and dwelt among is ambiguity itself. Ambiguity is also what the Word became when it became flesh, if we are to take seriously the theologians' assertions that the Christ was fully human.

As Paul Tillich pointed out in his *Systematic Theology,* our quest for God is always ambiguous, because it is carried on in finite moral and cultural terms. Most of us would agree that there is nothing sacred and unambiguous about at least some of those cultural terms: the altar guild, male clergy, the size and number of the communion cups, potluck suppers, or "debts" instead of "trespasses." But, potentially absurd though some of the cultural terms of religion are, most of them at least some of the time, in spite of their limitations, have helped us discover and celebrate the Holy. In a similar way, a dance is a humanly created structure through which we may perceive some part, large or small, of the meaning of our lives. Not in itself sacred, a dance can give us newly awakened bodies and minds with which to perceive and celebrate God–with–us in the world.

Those of us making art in religious contexts will do well to remember the question the angels asked the disciples after the Ascension. As the writer of Acts tells it, the astonished disciples stand gaping at the sky; you get the feeling they would like to build a chapel—or at least a wayside shrine—on the spot where they last saw Jesus. But two angels interrupt their reverie: "Why are you standing here staring at the sky?" (Acts 1:11, LB). The implication seems to be, "Get on with the business at hand," which is, of course, the business of being the church visible and active in the world. Contemporary choreographers who want to make dances for the church might take this text as a touchstone, making pieces that help us to look, with eyes wide open, at the daily mystery of here and now.

SUMMARY

Music and dance can attend to basic human questions that in turn become basic theological questions. How do I deal with my past? (How can my own involvement with evil be forgiven?) How do I deal with my present? (How do I learn to love my neighbor?) How do I deal with my future? (How do I face finitude and death?) Igor Stravinsky concluded his Harvard lectures, *Poetics of Music,* with this comment:

For the unity of the work has a resonance all its own. Its echo, caught by our soul, sounds nearer and nearer. Thus the consummated work spreads abroad to be communicated and finally flows back towards its source. The cycle, then, is closed. And that is how music comes to reveal itself as a form of communion with our neighbor—and with Being.[5]

Biblically rooted music and dance deepen our knowledge of God, ourselves, and each other. Composers and choreographers working in religious settings or with religious material are creating and presenting theological images. These nonverbal statements have great power to shape our understanding and action—often greater power than verbal communications have. This is why it is a mistake to understand the arts in the church as simply a matter of aesthetics, unless by aesthetics we mean the fleshing out of a vision of reality.

The arts direct us away from system and answer toward a relational theological process. The only way to know an art-work is to wait: to wait with, wait for, wait on the intuitive truth it has to tell. This process of waiting, watching, listening creates in the one who waits an empty space into which some new perception of the truth can come.

One of the most valuable things about the arts is that they unblushingly tell us so many diverse truths. Because they do this, they encourage us to break the idols—political, theological, personal—we make for ourselves. They remind us that if we are to first image and then create a more just future for the church and the world, flexibility will be a keystone of the whole structure.

Which means learning to live in and with ambiguity. The arts remind us that we never "know" God, or very much else, fully, and that the physical world is the only theater of revelation. Too often, dance and music in the church have been like those bright and appealing posters with puppies and kittens and relentlessly optimistic religious sayings, which we so often see in religious sales catalogues. But one of those poster series includes a picture of a howling child with a bowl of spaghetti upside down on his head. The caption is, "Wherever two or three are gathered together, someone spills the milk."

At least part of the business of the arts in the church is to reflect—and invite us deeper into—the ambiguity that is the natural habitat of human beings. Somewhere in the interior of that landscape stands the stable of Bethlehem, where the word became flesh and dwelt among us.

St. Mark's Dance Company in Carnival, by Barbara Wright-Craig. Left to right: Rosetta Brooks, Ronald Taylor, Julie Craighill, Karl Boykin, Marilyn Hamilton. Photo: Pat Field

Chapter 3

Moses and the Burning Bush

The Choreographer's Encounter

A seminarian once asked Frederick Buechner where the characters in his novels come from. He replied, "Probably from the same place dreams come from." There is a sense in which we do not "think up" the characters and images of artworks, just as we do not "think up" our dream images. They arrive quickly or slowly, hazy or fully formed, from the image-making depths of ourselves. Suddenly, there they are, standing in the shadowy doorways of our interior spaces.

This is perhaps the most mysterious thing about a dance, or any artwork: where it comes from. How does an idea, a feeling, or a design concept become a dance? How does the choreographer know which ideas, feelings, and design studies can be made into dances? It is surprising that Christians and others whose traditions are grounded in the Bible have not given more attention to this mysterious creative journey that we find in the arts and, in other ways, in all human effort. As Dorothy Sayers pointed out in *The Mind of the Maker,* the first image for God that the Bible offers us is the image of Creator.[1] "In the beginning God created the heavens and the earth" (Gen. 1:1). Although most translations of the passage go on to use the masculine pronoun for God, the central image itself, Creator, is an analogy with human activity that points equally to men and women. These opening words of the Bible invite us to find out what the human artist does, in order to discover something about the nature and action of God. Although this inclusive image has not been much explored in contemporary theology, it offers a rich mine of new and nonsexist insight into the nature of God and of human beings. It is essential that the women's movement in the church find imagery that goes beyond the female body and birth, because many women do not personally experience being pregnant and giving birth. Though that imagery can be helpful and important, it is also exclusive—as, of course, are *all* images. Nonetheless, to be made in God's image means that each of us is, by definition, a maker of things. As the church encounters artists at work, unique opportunities are created for the "doing" of theology in response to the work and insights of these individual creators.

The details of the creative process vary greatly, but for each creator the beginning of a new work is the beginning of a journey. One way to gain insight into a new process or idea is to clothe it in familiar imagery; that imagery becomes a paradigm that can yield deeper understanding of the new process. The story of Moses and the burning bush in the first chapters of Exodus offers us a paradigm for the process of artistic creation, although the biblical story is not, in its context, about the work of creating. This is the story itself:

Now Moses was keeping the flock of his father-in-law, Jethro, the priest of Midian; and he led his flock to the west side of the wilderness, and came to Horeb, the mountain of God. And the angel of the Lord appeared to him in a flame of fire out of the midst of a bush; and he looked, and lo, the bush was burning, yet it was not consumed. And Moses said, "I will turn aside and see this great sight, why the bush is not burnt." When the Lord saw that he turned aside to see, God called to him out of the bush, "Moses, Moses!" And he said, "Here am I." Then [God] said, "Do not come near; put off your shoes from your feet, for the place on which you are standing is holy ground." [Exod. 3:1–5]

If we remove the story from its context and retell it with the choreographer in the role of Moses and the idea for a dance in the role of the burning bush, we learn several things about how a dance is made. First, we see that the choreographer discovers the dance idea just as Moses encountered the amazing bush: in the process of doing something else. It is important to notice that Moses does not see the burning bush in Egypt, but elsewhere, and while he is doing something apparently irrelevant to the problem of Israel's slavery: keeping sheep. In other words, he has not single-mindedly set out to solve the problem of how to free his people. He is not out combing the mountainside for burning bushes—or even freedom fighters.

For some mysterious reason, the choreographer, like Moses, often discovers revelation while doing something besides choreographing. This simultaneity of experience, which so often leads to insight, seems to be especially noticeable in the lives of women, mystics, and artists. It is related to the "waiting with" stance toward events discussed in the previous chapter. Women have traditionally nearly always done more than one thing at a time: minding children, making soup, planting the garden, talking to a friend, making a quilt. This very ordinary and often difficult fact of feminine life teaches a receptive stance toward new experience; it offers richness to the perceptive possibilities of contemporary women and men in institutional roles as well as in personal life. This is because simultaneous activity seems to create a flexible interior space where there is room for creativity and revelation. The new idea makes room for itself while one is walking the dog, riding in an airplane, driving alone at night, typing a letter.

Moses saw the bush while herding sheep. If the choreographer in our paradigm is like Moses, what are the "sheep" for whom he or she is responsible? They are the surprising and unruly elements of the creative imagination, collected from here, there, and everywhere, and not necessarily having anything to do with dance. My own flock of sheep includes *Alice in Wonderland,* W. H. Auden's poems, the threat of nuclear war, the color of the sky just before dark, dreams about water, a joke about pigs, the pains of adolescence, cartoons from *the New Yorker,* a red fox seen in a cornfield at noon, an art exhibit about angels, the experience of being tear-gassed, my grandmother's wedding picture, lop-eared rabbits, and on and on. I have not consciously selected these sheep to be part of my flock; they have simply gathered. Every artist is involved in an endless process of feeling, noticing, and remembering. For some, the process is focused more on the external world of things and people; for others, more on the internal world of thoughts and feelings. It is this unlikely "flock of sheep," tended and increased constantly, that provides the occasion for the often surprising idea for a new work.

For example, a solo called *A Dance of Death* emerged from the gathering of elements from this internal collection around an external life event. The event was a dance injury, and the "sheep" were the experience of seeing two bones used as percussion instruments; the memory of female TV stars of the 1950s making swishing entrances through doors and down staircases; and the color red. The dance is about a woman's confrontation with various "deaths," and includes two cow rib-bones used by the dancer as design elements. The costume is a dramatic red evening gown. Interwoven with the sound-track are several of my own poems, which intensify the feminine imagery I have attempted to create around the idea of death. One poem is about the small death of re-jection—and also, I have since seen, about the contrast between the traditionally masculine and the traditionally feminine ways of being.

> *For her lover*
> > *a woman made,*
> > > *from one lily*
> > > > *and a quanity of red ink,*
> *an illuminated manuscript.*
> *The bookkeeping alone*
> *was daunting,*
> *and the lily screamed*
> *whenever it was touched.*
> *the lover—*
> > *he of the gift—*
> > > *is now the President of the Bank of* _____
> *and she is the curator*
> *of a very small museum.*

As they did in *A Dance of Death,* the choreographer's "sheep" may be said to create the context for the discovery of the "burning bush"—that is, an idea for a dance. Sometimes one can pinpoint the exact time and place when a particular dance became a possibility. Other times what happens in the identifiable moment is the clarifying of an idea that has been half-consciously present in various stages for a long time. A dance called *Mary Alice's Magnificat* emerged very suddenly for me during a plane trip, as I was looking out of the window and thinking about my grandmother, whose name was Mary Alice. That thought suggested Mary's Song of Praise in the Bible; and the idea, to make a dance about my grandmother as an Appalachian woman of strong religious faith, presented itself. *Wrestling with the Angel* is an example of the second way dance ideas sometimes emerge. In 1976, I began, for no particular reason, to imagine a performing space, diagonally divided by some sort of barrier, as the setting for a dance about crossing or not crossing barriers, boundaries, and obstacles. In the course of the next six years, the diagonal barrier mentally evolved into a folding chair, and the emotional atmosphere of the Bible story of Jacob wrestling at the Jabbok stream became part of the image; finally, in 1982, I began work on the duet that became *Wrestling with the Angel*.

But whether what happens in the identifiable moment is the sudden emergence of a completely new dance idea, or the final clarifying of one that has been present for some time, the moment is a wonderful one for the choreographer. Elated at the new idea, the choreographer feels that not only the dance idea, but everything, is clear, satisfying, and right. There is a sense of completeness and fulfillment, a sense of "Ah, *this* is what I have been waiting for!" The idea seems perfect, without flaw or difficulty; carrying it out seems the work of a moment.

The Bible does not tell us how Moses felt when God told him that Israel was going to be freed from slavery. Perhaps the reason is that Moses' opportunity for feeling ecstatic was brief. Before he had a chance to say anything, he discovered that this revelation meant work, trouble, and seeming foolishness. He learned that his glorious vision on the mountainside required him to tell the King of Egypt that unless he let Israel go free, God was going to make it rain frogs. Moses, understandably, was reluctant.

51

The choreographer sometimes feels that his or her task is about as sensible as asking for an audience with Pharaoh in order to give him the news about the frogs. The new and compelling idea leads to work, trouble, and seeming foolishness. Like Moses, the choreographer has to take the vision from the mountain to the city, from the internal world of images and perfection into the external world of people, things, and limitations. This is the only way the moment of revelation can become a force and an event for other people.

The vision on the mountain sent Moses to Egypt to confront Pharaoh and rally the Israelites, but he did not have to go alone; Aaron went along to interpret his vision. Neither does the choreographer go alone. Although the idea sends the dance creator into the studio to find dance movement for the new piece, it also sends him or her into relationship with other people who, as Aaron did for Moses' vision, help the new thing come to be and also change it by their presence.

The performing arts of dance, music, and drama are often more social in their making than are the visual arts. Because they usually depend on a large number of people for their production and vitality, the process of their making can be a source of insight for people in the faith traditions whose focus is on community. The new idea sends the choreographer into contracts and covenants with the dancers who will perform the new dance; into conversations with music librarians, record store managers, recording studio technicians, and musicians to find the right sound for the dance; into conversations and compromises with costume designers; and back into the studio with the dancers for weeks of rehearsal, editing, and reediting. Finally, the vision sends the choreographer and the dancers into a performing space—worship setting, social hall, or concert stage—where the dance meets the people for whom it was made: the audience.

This paradigm highlights four elements of the creative process that can be especially stimulating and freeing for a religious community. Each of these elements has important implications for a congregation.

1. Creating means trusting both the irrational and the rational parts of oneself.

2. Doing nothing can be an important part of the creative process.

3. The delight and satisfaction that come with the moment of creative insight are always followed by hard work.

4. The artist risks ridicule, failure, and misunderstanding with each new work.

Trusting the Irrational

One gift the choreographer brings to a religious community is that he or she allows others to see the results, successful and unsuccessful, of trusting the irrational or nonlogical parts of the creating self. In order to make something new, the unthinkable has to be tried. This seems obvious enough when we think of the arts, but it is sometimes difficult for us to affirm in a religious context. Art, by definition, tends to thrive on the new, the surprising, even the outrageous thing. But because religion has such a large element of essential tradition, because many people turn to their faith not for challenge but for comfort, and because some ideas of reverence are physically stifling, the exuberantly new is often not welcome in the sanctuary. It cannot be said too often, however, that God's presence and word are usually discovered in surprising places and things. The prophet tells the astonished and insulted citizens of Jerusalem that their deadly enemy, Assyria, is God's chosen instrument of punishment. The devout Paul, trying to stamp out what he regards as a heretical new sect, becomes its most ardent member. God's word becomes flesh in an ordinary man, the carpenter Jesus. But now that those events are objects of reverence, we don't usually think of them as things that were, when they happened, scandalous to many religious people. We hesitate to welcome the new, the unusual, the untried creation into our worship and religious education, but if we were really "traditional," that is just what we *would* do!

The choreographer's leap of faith in giving new dances a chance can be a contemporary reminder to us that God is to be found in what we haven't yet done, thought, or felt. To recognize that God's word is not static, not wholly contained in any single human activity, event, style, or moment, is to let God be God—and to let us be human beings.

Each new dance is a potential illuming of some facet of our human experience, a spotlight turned on some new place where we might meet each other and God. Trusting the irrational, nonlogical parts of the creative process allows the choreographer to make new combinations of ideas and insights that open our eyes and ears to old truths, new possibilities, and the creation around us. This means that there is a place in education, worship, and other religious settings not only for dances that are clearly "about" deep human and religious realities, but also for dances that are design studies and for dances that are simply humorous entertainment. To be able to appreciate the beauty and skill of the dancing human body and to be able to laugh uproariously are worthwhile accomplishments. Dance that falls into these two categories can have a special value in a religious setting, and for two reasons. First, because we have a biblical mandate to celebrate God's creation, pronounced by its Creator to be good. And second, because appreciating, enjoying, and learning from dance that is not "about" an issue or story gives us additional practice in using and trusting the nonlogical, nonverbal part of ourselves. All our relationships, including our relationship with God, are enhanced and deepened by that learning.

Trusting the nonrational or nonlogical part of the creating self means learning to be extravagant for whatever one cares deeply about. Artists know that if their art is to flourish, they must be willing to be extravagant, not only with money and materials, but also with time and commitment, and in the scope of their thinking. I once made a dance, called *House of Prayer,* that needed four enormous and expensive Hebrew letters as a stage set. Having the letters, one of which was seven feet tall, meant renting a truck in which to move them every time the dance was performed, and finding a place to store them when it was not being performed. One extravagance often leads to another; but we learn to live with the consequences, trusting the inner images and demands that are part of bringing a new thing to be in the world. There are times when a religious community needs to encourage its members to what may seem like foolish extravagances in the service of justice, truth, peace, and personal development. Artists can make good role models for learning the value of not counting the cost!

Trusting the nonlogical can also mean discovering the communicative power of nonsense: non sense. Body and Soul Dance Company began to discover the importance of non sense during the creation of *3-in-1-and-1-in-3,* about the Christian belief in the Holy Trinity. The dance uses both movement and words to make its point that theological language, for all its precision, cannot keep up with the mystery of God, and that the mystery of God is a relational reality in constant motion as God acts in the world. During one rehearsal break, the dancers began playing with the "tr" sound of the word *Trinity.* Soon the studio was filled with laughter as dancers declaimed: "Travel on trains is terrific . . . unless you're troubled by Tristram's traumatic tragedy . . . or treed by troops of Trappists." Nonsense, to be pushed aside with a shake of the head and a frown for its "irreverence"? No, non sense, something *besides* sense —something *else,* with its own value and possibility. These phrases and others were eventually used in the dance as a way of saying that although we don't often admit it, formal theological language sometimes makes as much "sense" to us as "treed by troops of Trappists" does. The point of the dance is that although a logical understanding of our tradition is part of the truth and of our task, it is probably wiser not to take our logical and theo-logical formulations as the last word about reality.

Receptivity Versus Activity

Doing nothing is an essential part of the creative process. It is important to notice that the Incarnation itself took place through the willingness of Mary to sit still, receive, "do" nothing. In so many paintings of the Annunciation, Mary is at rest, passive and receptive. This is a difficult image for most of us. Men have traditionally been required to be aggressive and decisive; women have discovered that we have the same capacity for active worldshaping. But, however important action may be, the silent, often motionless Mary of these paintings witnesses to the importance of being willing to do nothing so that revelation can happen. Non-doing has been, in our culture, a traditional female role, and one that, for many reasons, is in particularly bad repute these days. Nevertheless, we need to reexamine the close relationship between nondoing and new life. Artists can help both women and men to embrace the receptive, intuitive, noncontrolling parts of themselves, and to use the gifts these personal depths offer.

This may be an especially important point for Calvinist Protestants. Brought up to feel that our action for good in the world is necessary and important, some of us simply cannot bring ourselves to do nothing. Many church people cannot, for example, organize a conference with even a few hours of completely free time on the agenda. Yet to allow totally unstructured time is essential for the emergence of anything genuinely new. We do not, like God, create from nothing. We create by putting ideas, insights, colors, movements, sounds, and so on together in new ways, so that things not seen before emerge from familiar elements. To allow those new collisions and mergers to happen, we need to be alert to messages from the depths of ourselves, and we need to *look,* to simply see the world around us. Constant busyness, even work-related busyness intended to enable this process, is nonfunctional. We become not only unable to hear the messages from our depths, but unable even to know that we need to hear and see.

If a church community comes to understand and respect this periodic nonactivity of the artist, the whole community may acquire a new appreciation for the nonactivity of the contemplative side of Christianity. It is not a coincidence that the Protestant tradition has tended to devalue both contemplation and artistic creation. Understanding nondoing as part of the creative process of the choreographer in the congregation's midst can lead to greater understanding of the nondoing that is part of religious contemplation.

Reflecting on the nondoing that is necessary for creation also has implications for the way the artist is asked to work in the religious setting. The congregation comes to realize that casually asking the choreographer to make a new dance for "two weeks from Sunday" is not usually a sensible request. Authentic work is rarely produced on that sort of schedule, and the congregation cheats itself of its chance to encounter excellent dance.

Delight and Satisfaction—Then Hard Work

The fact that the artist's moment of insight always leads to work and difficulty suggests a somewhat alternative view of human work. We are accustomed to say, both sociologically and theologically, that *satisfying* work is necessary for the full dignity and development of human beings. This is an improvement over the older view of work as part of the lamentable fate of humankind, forced to get its living by the sweat of its brow as the punishment for sin. But we can go further and understand work itself as a signal part of what it means to be made in the image of One whom the biblical writer presents laboring for six days at the work of creation.

All of us are, by definition, creators in various ways, because we are made in the Creator's image. But some people, misunderstanding what the artist does, devalue this dimension of their identity. The obvious creativity of the writer, painter, composer, or choreographer is often taken as the model for all human creating. The problem with this is that many people have never watched an artist at work, or even talked with one about the process of making a novel, a painting, a symphony, or a dance. For some reason, perhaps our cultural reliance on technology, we tend to feel that creators are those for whom production is easy; if we ourselves find it hard to make a pot or a poem or a dance, we must not be creators. So the act of making is rejected, seen as belonging only to a special segment of the population known as "artists." The truth is that we may indeed not be potters or poets or choreographers, but that does not mean we are not creators.

57

One way to help people reclaim this crucial part of their identity is to bring a secure and articulate professional choreographer into a congregation for a residency. He or she is commissioned to create a dance for some event in the congregation's life. A period of time is set for the work (perhaps two to three months), dancers are recruited, and a rehearsal schedule is set. Groups from the congregation attend rehearsals as observers; talk with choreographer and dancers, in church-school classes and other places, about the experience of making the dance; and reflect together on the biblical story of creation, and on parallels between the creative process they are observing and various kinds of creation in their own lives. The congregation sees the choreographer and dancers in all phases of the work: frustrated and pleased, stuck and "cooking," tired and excited. They see the dance evolve into a reality and notice the ways it changes as it grows, including the way it is affected by the choreographer's growing knowledge of and relationship with the congregation. They watch the choreographer decide which choreographic limitations to accept and which to fight. These limitations include his or her own imaginative limits, various limitations of the dancers' body structure and technique, and also limitations imposed by the idea, the space, the music, and the budget.

As has been stated, one special dimension of the choreographic process is that it happens through a community: the dancers, the choreographer, and often musicians and stage technicians, who have to discover how to work with each other to bring the dance into being. The congregation sees that dance is a community event, not only because it is intended to communicate to an audience, but also because it is usually brought into being by a group of people who create it through service, discipline, and covenant. The personal and theological reflection resulting from following a dance from conception to presentation can therefore illumine not only the fact that individuals are creators, but also the way in which a congregation is a creator as its members work together to learn, grow, and make a difference in their community and in the world.

Risks of the Process

The artist risks ridicule, failure, and misunderstanding each time he or she presents a new work. As a congregation interacts with choreographers and their work over a period of time, a new appreciation for the risks of creation can develop, along with greater ease in giving each other permission to fail. Sometimes a dance, despite a seemingly good idea and hard work, just never "works out" or "comes right." Because dance is a performing art, some of a choreographer's failures and some of a dancer's failures take place in front of an audience. This is an opportunity for a congregation to develop a theology of failure. Is success a mark of God's favor? As religious people, do we accept our culture's compulsive demand for success? If not, why not, and what do we put in its place? What gifts of freedom for the future do we give each other when we give permission to fail?

Audience members have taught me, as both choreographer and performer, that although no dance is perfect, many dances, in spite of their imperfections, offer insight and challenge to those who see them. Learning this means receiving and processing both positive and negative feedback—and learning to distinguish between negative feedback and failure.

Sometimes, audience members' comments come as overwhelming affirmations of one's work. A chaplain in a convalescent hospital told me that serving communion there would never be the same after seeing *Mary Alice's Magnificat,* the dance about my grandmother's life and death. He said the dance had given him a glimpse of what it meant to be an eighty-year-old widow, reflecting on a long life and facing death, with the communion of saints very close indeed. After seeing this same piece, a young dancer responded, "Now I know why I go to class and do my pliés." A minister's wife contemplating divorce responded with tears and recognition to *St. Peter's Wife,* a dance about those who are left behind, intentionally or not, when someone "goes running off into the Holy." After a performance of *Wrestling with the Angel,* a church

MOSES AND THE BURNING BUSH

musician commented that he felt freer to take some risks in his life after watching the performers' apparent enjoyment of the physical risks taken in the dance.

Then there are the other kinds of responses. *A Dance of Death,* already partially described, ends with the dancer holding the two curving bones like a ballerina's postperformance bouquet, while the recorded contralto laughter of a woman echoes through the space. This final image sometimes unsettles and alienates audiences. At the dance's conclusion, one church audience sat motionless, refusing to applaud, simply glaring at me until I exited the space. During a discussion after another performance of this piece, someone asked, "Why did you show us *that?*" On another occasion, a group of politically and theologically conservative Latin American women took me severely to task after seeing my *Madre Tierra, Madre Lucha,* about the struggle of Guatemalan peasants for justice and peace. Experiences and comments like these force the choreographer to listen, discern, and reflect carefully. They are, among other things, occasions for deciding whether one is irrevocably committed to one's personal vision or not. They represent an essential stage of growth for the creator of dances.

There are also the "bucket of cold water" comments, from critics or audience members, which shrewdly challenge the choreographer or dancer to make the next developmental leap. I will never forget being literally backed up against a wall by an unknown woman at a party in San Antonio, after a performance of *Baptism,* and told, "You're nervous when you dance. You don't need to be. Stop it; it gets in the way." She was right, and I began then and there trying to let go of my personal version of stage fright, because whatever gets in the way of the dance *has* to be let go.

Mountainside, Pharaoh's court, wilderness, and promised land: the biblical burning bush sent Moses and his community on a long journey indeed. The small and particular "burning bush" that is a dance idea also sends choreographer, dancers, and audience on a journey. It is a journey taken in laughter and tears to discover more about who we are, whose we are—and where we are going!

THE COMPOSER'S ENCOUNTER

The story of Moses and the burning bush as a paradigm for the creating artists do becomes even more provocative if we realize that it is really the story of Moses and Aaron and the burning bush. Looking at the story as paradigm, and also looking at the way the story itself has been used as a subject for musical composition, illumines the process of composition.

Coming from the earliest memories of biblical writers, the story of Moses' encounter presents the composer as well as the choreographer with an impressive analogy for the creative process in all its authority and ambiguity. For Moses, the flame of new vision came unexpectedly in the ordinary routine of life. The fire that did not destroy what it burned was a source of self-discovery, inspiration, and new direction.

Musicians work routinely with common materials: piano keys with hammers hitting tightly stretched wires; violin bows with hair sending gutstrings into motion; pipes whose inside air is set vibrating by human breath; microcomputers providing instant permutations of sound. They are materials that follow predictable physical laws. Yet in the midst of that ordinariness, the unexpected happens; like Moses, the composer sees something not seen before and turns aside to discovery. Precisely in that turning aside lies the beginning of a new creation.

Composers frequently comment upon this sudden opening of new directions. Paul Hindemith likened it to "a very heavy flash of lightning in the night."[2] In 1950, Hindemith wrote, "We experience a view immensely comprehensive and at the same time immensely detailed, that we never could have under normal daylight conditions."[3] Ten years earlier, Stravinsky described the phenomenon in a different way: "In the course of my labors I suddenly stumble on something unexpected. This unexpected element strikes me. I make a note of it. At the proper time I put it to profitable use."[4] Seeing the fire and responding to it are primary in the creative process. The fire of inspiration gives a fundamental energy unrelated to logic.

Only energy from such a deep source can support the composer in the stumbling, depressing, exhilarating and absorbing task of creation. Because, as we have seen, once the new possibility has been glimpsed, it compels action. So much so that sometimes the composer feels like another biblical prophet, Jeremiah, who cursed the day he was born, saying, "There is in my heart as it were a burning fire shut up in my bones, and I am weary with holding it in, and I cannot" (Jer. 20:9).

Having once turned aside to investigate the new idea, the composer is faced with a bewildering array of choices. Like all creators, he or she must then proceed to bring a technical order out of a chaos of possibility. The composer may embrace diversities and rejoice in the random, or impose limits and rejoice in artificial parameters. Different creators construct radically different sonic worlds by the way they respond to the choices the new idea presents to them. For a composer such as John Cage, all sounds offer musical beginnings. It is in their order of succession that music becomes what it may. In an imaginary conversation with fellow composer Erik Satie, Cage wrote:

Nevertheless, we must bring about a music which is like furniture— a music, that is, which will be part of the voices of the environment, will take them into consideration. [Satie "speaking"]

Current musical activities involve . . . discovering and acting upon . . . all audible sounds in any combination and any continuity issuing from any points in space in any transformations. [Cage "speaking"]5

On the other hand, Stravinsky insisted upon tight control of all aspects of sound, limiting himself to the pitches of the Western chromatic scale. He said of the artist's task of making choices:

The more art is controlled, limited, worked over, the more it is free. . . . As for myself, I experience a sort of terror when . . . I have the feeling that everything is permissible to me. . . . I shall overcome my terror and shall be reassured by the thought that I have the seven notes of the scale and its chromatic intervals at my disposal, that strong and weak accents are within my reach, and that in all of these I possess solid and concrete elements which offer me a field of experience just as vast as the upsetting and dizzy infinitude that had just frightened me.[6]

Karlheinz Stockhausen has managed to combine both polarities of the random and the controlled in his music. His *Gesang der Jünglinge* (Song of the Three Young Men, 1956) uses a child's voice singing the cosmic praise of God. The voice was recorded, transformed through electronic filters, and then combined with other electronically produced sounds. Stockhausen planned a performance in the huge cathedral at Cologne, using five loudspeaker groups with considerable spatial separation. The drift of sound from one set of speakers to another was part of the musical experience. Everything was tightly controlled by the composer. Indeed, the multitrack tapes themselves became the "performers"; nothing was left for a musician to do in the usual sense. Later, when a recording was made, limiting the tracks to two, the disk itself became the "score." The music was unrepeatable by any other musical force. Apart from the composer and the necessary playback gear, no other human being was needed.

More than a decade later, in 1968, Stockhausen moved to the opposite pole. Setting out fifteen brief written texts, the composer asked small groups of instrumentalists to respond to the texts *and to one another* intuitively. The resulting *Aus den sieben Tagen* (From the Seven Days) provides no musical notation; everything is left to human interaction and response.

Within these contrasting parameters, Cage, Stravinsky, and Stockhausen have produced music with incredible flexibility and emotive content. For each, the flash of insight is integral to his understanding of the creative process, but each has handled the resulting choice-making differently, and the result is three very distinct musical styles. Reflecting on this diversity of method and result among creators is one of the stimulating reasons for helping religious communities to interact with art and artists. We begin to see that each human creator has a unique but limited vision. None sees or can work with all of the possibilities. Conceivably, if someone else—Moses' sister, Miriam, for example—had been the one to see the burning bush, some other story entirely would have come down to us! In this sense, the composer's journey of making is a powerful testimony to the inevitability and importance of differing visions of the possible—and therefore of reality.

However, as Stravinsky felt so vividly, the individual composer must choose from among these differing versions. By what authority, then, are the choices made? While Moses had no difficulty recognizing the God of his family in the flame of the burning bush, we are not so sure. Authority for many of us is hard to come by. Perhaps the crucial ingredient in our response to the unexpected lies in our willingness to be wrong. Choose we must, but at the same time we must risk the danger of the wrong turn, the dead end.

The composer is one very willing to risk having plans demolished, starting over again, seeking other solutions—and being artistically rejected. New musical choices require new responses from audiences, and audiences, like all of us much of the time, often do not want to make new and open responses. A recent review of some of Cage's music for Merce Cunningham's choreography illustrates this point. The reviewer likened the music to the sound of "sniveling bullfrogs."

The story of Moses and the burning bush suggests that the creator must trust the vision enough to be able to argue bitterly with it. A creative idea worth its salt has implications revealed only over time and in the process of intense relationship. Generally, as the idea's depth and the tasks it is going to impose on the artist become clear, the artist is, at points at least, appalled.

Once having revealed the divine imperative, God laid out a plan for Moses. He was to return to his own people in Egypt and lead them from there to "a land flowing with milk and honey" (Exod. 3:17). The story describes Moses' objections to all this work and risk and change:

Who am I that I should go to Pharaoh? . . . If I come to the people of Israel and say to them, "The God of your fathers has sent me to you," and they ask me, "What is his name?" what shall I say to them? . . . They will not believe me . . . for they will say, "The Lord did not appear to you." . . . Oh, my Lord, I am not eloquent . . . I am slow of speech and of tongue. . . . Oh, my Lord, send, I pray, some other person. [Exod. 3:11–4:13, condensed]

To each objection, God responds with help and increasing anger, finally appointing Aaron, Moses' brother, to speak in his place: "You shall speak to him and put the words in his mouth. . . . He shall speak for you to the people; and he shall be a mouth for you, and you shall be to him as God" (Exod. 4:15–16). Moses was the one with the vision, the person to whom the fire appeared, but another became the interpreter. Here the gap between idea and outcome becomes vividly apparent. It is a struggle faced by many composers. Between vision and reality lie not only seemingly endless work, discouragement, and self-doubt, but also the ultimate impossibility of communicating exactly and wholly one's vision to another. The tensions between Moses and Aaron are not unlike those between composer and performer.

One of the musical masterpieces of the 1930s is the extraordinary opera dealing with this issue of the gap between the one who has the vision and the one who interprets it: *Moses und Aron,* by Arnold Schoenberg. Having created his libretto, carefully based on the Exodus story, several years earlier, Schoenberg completed the first two acts by March 1932. A third act was planned but never finished.

In the difficult time between two world wars, here was one composer who thoroughly understood the creative questions of authority, ambiguity, and resistance. Schoenberg, born in 1874 in Vienna, grew up in a Jewish family, became a Christian in the early part of his life, then returned to Judaism in Paris in 1933, having resigned his teaching position in Berlin in protest against the growing anti-Semitism there. A letter to the painter Kandinsky in 1923 foreshadowed his action: "I have at last learned the lesson that has been forced upon me during this year, and I shall not ever forget it. It is that I am not a German, not a European . . . but I am a Jew."[7] In another letter to his student and friend Alban Berg, he wrote: "Today I am proud to call myself a Jew; but I know the difficulties of really being one."[8] *Moses und Aron* opens with the calling of Moses from the burning bush. Even before the curtain rises, the music begins with the voice of God: three women and three men, singing very softly with the orchestra. What they sing is a stunning characterization of the divine. On the open vowel "O," each group of soloists presents three-note chords, three beats in duration, that spread across three measures. The women's sonority is the mirror image of the men's, with the first and last chords being the same. This unusual sound is never heard again in the entire work, but it opens our ears to a symmetric unity, the One who is infinite. The curtain rises and we next hear Moses acknowledging the great "O": "Only One, infinite, thou omnipresent One, unperceived and inconceivable God!" Schoenberg provides Moses, he who "is not eloquent," with pitchless sounds controlled only by speed and rhythm. In the music, Moses is described as a "deep resounding voice" with any difference in pitch serving only to emphasize the declamation.

God (the six soloists) from the burning bush then commands Moses, "Be God's prophet!"

"I am old," says Moses, "let me tend my sheep in peace."

God tells him, "You have seen your people enslaved; you have known the truth. You can do nothing else; you must set your people free!"

The familiar story of vocational resistance is retold, with Moses finally, and sadly, pointing out, "I can think, but I cannot speak." Then Aaron is given as his helper, and his people are promised God's leading. Schoenberg adds to the text: 'They are the people of the one God alone. They are thus to know him and to worship him alone. They will undergo all hardships that through millennia have ever come to be conceived" (act I, scene 1).

With the first scene completed in all its restrained power and penetrating insight, the composer begins the second scene with music of an entirely different quality. Aaron arrives in the midst of lively, lilting sounds. He greets Moses with an overly grand musical gesture in wide intervals and obvious rhythms; the words are superfluous: "O son of my father!" In less than a minute, Schoenberg makes it painfully clear that the gap between vision and interpretation is going to be sizable. Aaron may know how to market an idea but he has little understanding of the idea itself. The tragic dilemma is before us. Moses, who understands the idea, cannot articulate it, and therefore must live with the warped interpretations Aaron will give it. Of course, this is not always the case between composer and performer. But the developing situation between Moses and his brother, Aaron, underscores the contrast that always lies between the conception of an idea and its implementation. The implementation may be glorious—but it is never identical with the conception.

Aaron seems exclusively interested in the magic powers of God and how best to manipulate the people to accept those powers and do what Moses, through him, urges. Aaron seeks overt evidence of God's cosmic control and of God's promise to the Israelites. In brief, Aaron expresses the "image" of the idea in concrete, limited terms. The last music of the opera (act II, scene 5) is that of Moses calling out in despair: "Inconceivable God! Inexpressible, many-sided idea, will you let it be so explained? Shall Aaron, my mouth, fashion this image? Then I have fashioned an image, too: false, as an image must be."9

And yet Aaron is responding to the possibilities of Moses' vision and making choices—though they are choices Moses deplores. Every vision unleashes an apparently endless chain of response and new creation. One is reminded of Cage's description of Schoenberg's teaching at the University of California (Los Angeles) before World War II:

During a counterpoint class, Schoenberg sent everybody to the blackboard. We were to solve a particular problem he had given and to turn around when finished so that he could check on the correctness of the solution. I did as directed. He said, "That's good. Now find another solution." I did. He said, "Another." Again I found one.

Again he said, "Another." And so on. Finally I said, "There are no more solutions." He said, "What is the principle underlying all of the solutions?"10

"Inexpressible, many-sided idea." The fire of the burning bush for Moses, the flash of lightning in the night for Hindemith, the sudden stumble upon the unexpected for Stravinsky: all are attempts to describe the call of a creator and to understand the resulting struggle to convey new insights to others through a particular form, making one's peace with the inner conflict that necessarily arises in the shaping of reality to embody an original vision.

Recognition and response. Authority and ambiguity. Resistance and integrity. In the story of Moses and Aaron and the burning bush, they are fundamental to the divine-human encounter. They are fundamental also to the creative process of both creator and interpreter, and to their collaboration.

SUMMARY

Examining the creative process of choreographer and composer in relation to this biblical story highlights several ideas. First among them is that the encounter with creative energy is in many ways a chance encounter; it appears as the unexpected in the midst of ordinary experience. This moment of vision may feel like (and even be) holy ground, but the process of bringing the new thing to be is a matter of effort, persistence, and endless decision making. The serious artist is one who is up to the elbows in the stuff of God's world.

Creating means welcoming some traditionally "feminine" ways of being in the world. These include appreciating how simultaneous activity sets the stage for new insight; being willing to do nothing so that a vision can emerge; and being willing to appear impractical, extravagant, even foolish, so that a new work can be created. This seeming frivolity—an age-old charge against women and artists—is actually the surprisingly implacable energy that wrests from our practical world the time and space new visions need. The woman with a child, the artist attempting to embody a new vision, are both mothering something. Both can seem harassed, aimless, silly, blindly shortsighted, and exasperatingly absorbed in their progeny. But their stubbornness and commitment give the world new life and new vision.

When the artist responds to the unexpected idea or possibility, he or she is willing to turn aside from the usual and attend to the unlooked-for appearance: Hindemith's "heavy flash of lightning in the night." The courage to do this comes from trusting both the rational and nonrational parts of oneself. Any new idea always contains energy unrelated to logic.

To respond willingly is to risk gladly. New possibilities are vast and sometimes frightening. Like Moses in his response to the divine encounter, the creator is willing to test, to resist, to be misinterpreted, and to fail. Perhaps an identifying mark of the creative person is an openness to error, to wrong turns, to dead ends.

To stand before unlimited possibility is to stand before chaos. In order to be communicated, chaos must become form. It may be that this intentional opening of oneself to the chaos of possibility, besides being a characteristic of both artists and parents, is an ancient link between artist and shaman. Both go alone into mysterious places and come back to their communities with new wisdom, with a new glimpse of truth. The artist's insight may be small or large, but if a work is authentic, it becomes a living insight added to its audience's world of images and potential action.

However, there often seems a great gap between the original vision and the final outcome. The dilemma of the performing arts is the communal nature of the finished product. In some ways, a dance or a piece of music is never "finished," because there are always other performances by and for new people, and these influence and even shape the work. Moses and Aaron must make their peace with one another if the vision is to live and have results in the world.

Carla De Sola in her From the Diary of Anne Frank. *Photo: Beverly Hall*

Chapter 4

Performer as Priest and Prophet

IMAGE FOR THE MUSICIAN

Performers, in worship? Priests and prophets we already associate with the church's worship, and we expect to find them in the Sunday-morning cast, whether as actual worship leaders or as characters in readings from the Bible. But what do priests, prophets, and performers have to do with each other?

Although the church acknowledges a tradition of brilliant musical performers, such as Bach, Handel, and Mozart, and although churchgoers listen to musical presentations by choir and organist or other instrumentalists during most church services, we tend to reject the concept of performance in worship. Yet we often speak of a secular performer with high praise: an actress who moved us to tears; a string quartet that held us in awed silence; a dancer who danced Juliet so well that we discovered more about the tragedy of Shakespeare's story. If we listen to what we say about those who move us in religious settings, we realize that our praise sounds very similar: a preacher who touched us deeply; a reader who made a difficult passage in the Bible live; an organist who made us want to clap with joy. Where, then, and how, do the concepts of performance and worship meet?

Romano Guardini's *The Spirit of the Liturgy* suggests that one meeting point is in the realm of playfulness. In a chapter

71

called "The Playfulness of the Liturgy," Guardini quotes two
passages from the Bible, the first from Ezekiel's vision of the
four living creatures:

Each creature had two wings, each of which touched the wing of
another . . . and each went straight forward . . . wherever the spirit
would go, they went. . . . The living creatures darted to and fro, like
a flash of lightning. . . . They rose from the earth . . . the sound of
their wings like the sound of many waters. . . . When they stood still
they let down their wings. [Ezek. 1:11–]

Of them, Guardini writes,
"They are pure motion, powerful and splendid, acting
according to the direction of the Spirit, desiring nothing save
to express [the Spirit's] inner drift and its interior glow and
force. They are the living image of the liturgy."[1]
He then quotes the passage from Proverbs in which Wisdom describes how God created her:

When God's purpose first unfolded,
  before the oldest of God's works . . .
  when God laid down the foundations of the earth,
I was by God's side, a master crafter
  delighting God day after day,
  ever at play in God's presence,
at play everywhere in God's world,
  delighting to be with humankind. [Prov. 8:22, 30–31, JB
adapted]

Guardini concludes in a way that can illumine the issue of
performance and the emotional and intellectual responses it
creates:

In the earthly sphere, there are two phenomena which tend in the
same direction: the play of the child and the creation of the artist.
The soul . . . must learn . . . to play the divinely ordered game of
the liturgy in liberty and beauty and holy joy before God. [Liturgy]
is primarily concerned with reality, with the approach of a real creature

to a real God, and with the profoundly real and serious matter of redemption.[2]

Though the author is not talking directly about performance, he is suggesting that we need not be afraid of pleasure and delight and freedom when we worship. Indeed, he is saying that if those experiences and responses are missing, we will not be able to understand or participate in "the profoundly real and serious matter of redemption." We shy away from the idea of performance in liturgy because we shy away from the possibility of enjoyment in liturgy—especially the possibility of enjoying *ourselves*. We go to the theater to enjoy ourselves, not to church. But Guardini is asking us how we expect to "glorify God and enjoy God's presence forever" (as the Westminster Catechism puts it), if we refuse to enjoy in worship those who are made in God's image—ourselves and our fellow human beings? As performers in worship, musicians offer gifts that enable people to respond in wholeness, with heart, soul, mind, and strength, to the Holy.

To perform means to carry out, implement, and fulfill. Immediately, difficult questions about integrity and ability are raised. Among musicians, there is an old story about the pastor who sought out the organist to mention the awkward silence that occurred as the minister moved from lectern to pulpit. "Would you mind playing a few bars of music while I walk over?" "Sure; no problem," said the musician, "and just before the choir sings, there's a moment or two while singers stand up, find their music, open it, and get ready to begin. Would you mind mumbling a few words while we do that?" Webster tells us that *integrity* means "an avoidance of deception, expediency, artificiality, or shallowness of any kind." The integrity of all the arts that are part of worship is best preserved when no single one of them, including preaching, is regarded as "the star turn." The "real and serious matter of redemption" depends on our being moved, taught, and delighted by all of God's creation.

Ability is the other complex question that comes with the concept of performance. A musician spends years acquiring

73

facility with different dimensions of music: its performance, theory, and history. Many hours each week are spent in solitary practice as the musician confronts self-limitation and -worth. Doubt assails that person from all directions. "Will I ever be able to play this? Why can't I keep a steady beat? Do I really know what this music is all about? Will I ever fully understand it? Are my choices the right ones? What is 'right'?"

For performers at every level of expertise, there is no substitute for this kind of introspection, because doubts are yeasty challenges to the imagination. Doubts are painful means of keeping a keen edge on insight. Doubts are also pastoral channels that can lead to fruitful confrontations with one's own limits. In that recognition of finitude lies health and sanity. When a performer makes peace with personal limits, new possibilities and richness emerge. Is every composer a great composer? Is every organist a musical genius? Clearly not. Yet the biblical evidence suggests that divine purpose is carried forward by the least of humankind—that is, whenever the person called is willing to answer with the unstinting investment of gifts, energies, and time.

Peter Shaffer's recent play *Amadeus* shows Salieri, a successful composer, unable to accept his limits. In the first act, Salieri, having made a bargain with God (fame as a composer in return for serving God and humankind), is quite happy reaping the benefits of that bargain: a position as court composer in Vienna, the summit of musical power in the Hapsburg empire.

Then he meets Wolfgang Amadeus Mozart, and his life changes abruptly. The bargain is still intact; but Salieri now recognizes incredible talent enfleshed in a most unlikely youth newly arrived from the provinces. The gift is incarnational—of God, from God, freely given, with no bargain needed. Salieri tells us: "I was suddenly frightened. It seemed to me I had heard a voice of God—and that it issued from a creature whose own voice I had also heard—and it was the voice of an obscene child."[3]

Unable to accept his own limits, now made unbearably plain, Salieri declares war on God. It is too much to see genius in another, and through it to recognize one's own mediocrity. Act II details the downfall of the bargain: at every point, including a try at suicide, Salieri fails.

But mediocrity is where most performers exist: midway between extremes, neither brilliant nor excessively dull. One does one's best with the gift one is given. The point is that to say yes to that gift as it really is, is to say yes to its limits— and yes to the honest work that hones and polishes the gift. This is not the anxious, angry work that is really a denial of limits: "If I just do a little more, *then* I'll be able to. . . . " A Salieri can never become a Mozart. To say yes clears the air so that one can see and rejoice in things as they really are.

Clearing the air is in turn closely related to the performer's role as prophet. *Prophet* is a composite word from Greek, a combination of "pro" and "phētēs," a form of the verb "to say" or "to speak." A prophet is one who speaks for, on behalf of, clear visions of ultimate truth and reality: a divinely inspired revealer and interpreter whose clarity gives us fundamental insight into the nature of events.

In our society, it is often the artists who sense and dare to tell the only truth that matters, which is truth about the human condition and relationships. And musicians have often been in the forefront of sharing these prophetic, and therefore controversial, ideas. For example, to hear and see Mozart's opera *The Marriage of Figaro* is to understand more about the potential strength of people in apparently weak positions. Susanna, the maidservant of a countess, finds herself involved in a full-scale intrigue backed by the intricate web of power woven by the eighteenth-century nobility. Figaro, the manservant of a count, engaged to Susanna, is furious over the intrigue in which Susanna is forced to play a part. When Beaumarchais first produced the drama in 1784 (before it was redone by Mozart and his librettist, Da Ponte), he had to wade through considerable political intrigue himself; the Versailles court censors thought the play far too unsettling for the current establishment.

While the opera may well be seen as a blow aimed at privilege, it is more justly seen as a proclamation of two ideas that were prophetic in their time: that individuals should be rewarded for ability rather than birth, and that women are as capable as men and should be equally respected.

Mozart makes the first point clear in his matter-of-fact music for Figaro; he gives the listener a sonic picture of a competent human being who is quite prepared to turn established values and relationships upside down. The count's music, in contrast, is filled with bluster, with suggestions of bogus and unfulfillable power. The second point is made similarly clear by the music for both Susanna and the countess: the former clever and witty, the latter smooth with the controlled strength of one who has learned to rise above the silliness of her husband.

A recent example of music's capacity for unsettling and upsetting a community—this time not by social challenge but by artistic innovation—is what happened at the final session of the 1984 national meeting of the American Guild of Organists. At the closing gathering in St. Mary's Cathedral in San Francisco, *Orbits: A Symphonic Spatial Symphony for 84 Trombones and Organ,* by contemporary composer Henry Brant proved too much for some among this gathering of church musicians. As the sound from organ, soprano soloist, and the eighty-four trombones ranged around the church's perimeter crashed through the space, some AGO members angrily threw their thick conference programs at the feet of the conductor and walked out of the cathedral.

This incident underlines two points. One is that the musician as prophet challenges the limits we place on reality by making musical statements that confront and startle. The other is that the prophetic dimension of the church musician's role remains relatively undeveloped. This is partly because we have such an extensive and distinguished body of church music at our disposal: the work of Bach, Handel, and Mozart, among others. No matter how unexpected their work may have seemed in its own period, it is now, for us, "classical" and traditional. Their music "sounds like church" to us. Its sounds and patterns are familiar: we associate them with worship, and we expect to hear them in church. They represent for us some of the priestly music of the Christian tradition.

Our perception of such traditional "church music" suggests that what begins as prophetic often becomes priestly. Repetition, distance in time, and subsequent imitation by other artists take the edge off, so to speak, so that a piece of music that may originally have been heard as a sonic challenge becomes a reassuring old friend. Time, then, is part of the context that determines whether a work is experienced as prophetic or priestly.

The musician in a religious setting bears a responsibility for leading us out ("ēducāre") and calling us out ("ēvocāre") into new sonic and theological adventures. Not adventures we already know, but those not yet fully imagined. Apprehended, perhaps, rather than comprehended. Ralph Vaughan Williams, leading English composer of the first half of our century, stated this necessity in words that demonstrate, paradoxically, the pastoral dimension of prophetic challenge: "The composer must not shut himself up and think about art, he must live with his fellows and make his art an expression of the whole life of the community."[4]

The key words here are "the whole life of the community," implying for us that, perhaps especially in relationship to church music, we might do well to adopt Bach's attitude that there is no difference in principle between sacred and secular art. This attitude opens the worship space to the often dissonant and startling sounds and issues of our late-twentieth-century world.

However, the church musician's common reluctance to explore music's prophetic possibilities is in part a reflection of the situation in the musical world at large. Thoroughly new music is not standard fare in concert halls any more than it is in churches. Such music tends to be confined to special events or series. Perhaps the church itself, musical museum though it sometimes seems, can become a catalyst for a new opening to the prophetic dimension of music as church musicians take their prophetic responsibilities more seriously.

Though the musician's priestly role has been over-emphasized, it remains important. The musician who insists on new hymns or unfamiliar music for every service ignores the base of experience that allows for moving in any direction. *All* new means *nothing* new, because the framework of the relationship of old and new in time has been destroyed. Like the house built on sand rather than rock, the ritual activity of that musician's congregation has little connection with the support its musical past might provide. This prophetic dimension also has a priestly role in relation to other arts in the church. Because church musicians are usually so aware of the importance of music's past, music can, through them, challenge the other performing arts in the church to develop and maintain an awareness of their need for historical rootedness in community.

Prophet then, but also priest. The word is an old English contraction of the classical Greek "presbuteros." It meant "elder," one with responsibility within a community, one who presided over relationships within that community and worked to maintain the community's relationship with ultimate power. The priest is also a performer, implementing and fulfilling the historic, ritual activity of the community. The priest presents anew the traditions of the past that identify the particular group as it recalls, remembers, refreshes itself.

This is the predominant role twentieth-century musicians in the church generally play, but sometimes without the congregation's understanding of that role's potential and limits. Music increasingly has become a carrier of communal lore. Why, for instance, do we still sing the fourth-century hymns of Ambrose, which come out of a church whose burning theological issues and social concerns were in many ways so different from our own? One reason is that they allow us to participate in some of the deep insights and understandings of Christians of that time, reassuring us that those insights are also our own. Ambrose and his contemporaries in the faith understood that all time is in God's hands, and that all we do is made worthwhile by offering thanks and prayer. One song for the opening of the day asks that "Christ may be to us food and faith our drink, that we may with joy imbibe the sober drunkenness of the Spirit." "Give form to restless activity," Ambrose sings; "blunt the teeth of envy; rough misfortune change to good." Like the psalms, these hymns speak to the timeless human condition, acknowledging failure as well as hope.

Music ties us to our religious past whether or not we know its historical sequence. The plainchant of the medieval centuries, the Reformation's Psalm tunes, the vigorous Wesleyan melodies, the earnest, sometimes plaintive music of early American religious "awakenings": all these contribute to our sense of ourselves as a continuation of a living religious tradition. Our inheritance of church music might be said to play for us the role stained glass played for the illiterate believers of earlier centuries. It gives us a vivid physical confirmation of our religious identity.

Music is a foundation stone of our religious activity, and the musician who recognizes and makes available its power acts as both priest and prophet. When the community is reminded to be refreshed by our common memory, the Holy Spirit is discerned in the events of the past; then that same Spirit can be seen leading out those who say yes today into new adventure and fresh territory.

IMAGE FOR THE DANCER

Like the musician, the dancer in the church is also a performer called to play the dual roles of priest and prophet. *To perform,* according to the *Oxford English Dictionary,* means "to carry through *in due form,* accomplishing entirely" [emphasis mine]. A performer "carries through" by serving a form or craft, subordinating the self to it in order to communicate.

The dancer in worship joins the regular Sunday cast of more or less accomplished performers: people doing a certain thing in a certain way, to the best of their ability, singly or in groups, in order to communicate with watchers and listeners. In the Reformed churches, the star performer is the preacher (although worship experts debate about whether or not that ought to be the case). He or she has spent several years in seminary, plus the professional years in the parish, working at the art of homiletics and usually taking that art and its performance very seriously. In the more liturgical traditions, the celebrant or liturgist plays a more central role; many pastors and worship committees work long hours to carry out liturgies that are compelling and effective. Besides the clergy, there are the organist and choir director, who are often professional musicians. Many churches have paid choirs or soloists as well as unpaid choir members, and all of these rehearse at least weekly. In the course of worship the roles shift, of course, and the preacher becomes the choir's listener, the choir becomes the dancer's watchers, and so on. But all these people are performers, because they do a particular thing according to a particular form for others who watch and listen.

In order to "carry through in due form," the dancer must be skilled at the form served, which means meeting certain standards. The first of these is a thorough dance training. This points up the major difference between dance as a performing art in the church, and congregational or community dance. Technical dance training is not necessary for congregational movement or, for example, movement used within a prayer group as part of its meditation together. But training is essential for most dance done to be watched, in the church as well as in the theater, for the amateur as well as the professional. The dancer as performer is one who subordinates the self to the art of dancing, serving choreographic and technical forms so that communication can take place through a disciplined, articulate body. The professional accomplishes more virtuosic feats of technique, but the responsible amateur brings no less commitment to the craft of dance at his or her chosen level. Technique is essential, because the point of performance is not self-expression, the giving of the self to the watchers; the point is the giving of the *dance* to the watchers. Neither in the theater nor in the church can one get by on sincerity.

The second qualification for the dancer in the church is at least a basic musical knowledge, and the willingness to continue to grow musically. Some understanding of musical terminology and structure is necessary, as well as familiarity with a variety of musical periods and styles. One sure sign that the beginning dancer/choreographer needs more musical education is the creation of too many dances with similar music. Another indication of the need to broaden one's musical and choreographic horizons is overreliance on music with lyrics.

Choreographic training is essential for the dance performer in religious settings, because in these settings most dancers present their own, rather than someone else's, work. Because dance as a performing art in the church does not yet have a long history and a repertoire of masterpieces, the choreographic responsibilities of the dancer cannot be emphasized too much. If dance in the church is ever to have its masterpieces, it is up to contemporary dancers to create them, or at least to create a historical context whose integrity will support and feed the work of future artists.

Among the dancer's talents should also be inventiveness about costuming; alternatively, the dancer must find an imaginative and skilled costumer who can become a colleague. If the performer is to be the head of a group of dancers, directorial and administrative skills are also needed. And finally (not because it is the least important qualification, but because it is the most obvious one), the performer needs to understand and be stimulated by the possibilities dance offers to the church, and the church to dance. Dance in a religious context is always an interdisciplinary undertaking, bringing with it the need to grow continually in one's understanding of theology, spirituality, and worship.

As if acquiring all these skills were not enough, the dancer must learn to play the two distinct roles of priest and prophet: the role of priest, who consolidates, guards, and sanctions, reminding the community of its history, traditions, and achievements; and the role of prophet, who judges and challenges, reminding the same community of its failures and calling for a more righteous future. Because any viable artform is solidly rooted in history and geography, these two roles necessarily shift as the artist plays one and then the other, responding to events in the world and in the community's life. Both of these roles come to be reflected in the performer's repertoire and self-understanding. Because contemporary dance in the church does not have an extensive history and "classical" repertoire, it has the freedom to explore and emphasize its prophetic side—freedom perhaps less available to music, with its beloved repertoire from past centuries.

But what makes a dance prophetic? First, the setting in which it is done; second, its content and style. Being an Old Testament prophet does not seem to have meant simply mastering a body of material and saying it to anyone who came along. The prophets were concerned with speaking to people in particular situations. This means that a prophetic dance done for one congregation may or may not be perceived as prophetic when done for another congregation—or when done the next year for the original congregation. If a dance surprises us, challenges us, or helps us see something new, it may be, for that performance and in that place, prophetic.

For example, *Madre Tierra, Madre Lucha,* the piece mentioned earlier about Central American civil war, challenged two quite different groups within the international conference audience for whom it was created. After its first performance in 1982, many North Americans, unaware of disturbing events in Central America, reacted with interest, wanting to know what was going on there. Conservative Central Americans, on the other hand, criticized the dance company for presenting a work that questioned the status quo in their countries.

A choreographer takes risks when he or she presents a prophetic dance, because this kind of work often meets with anger and rejection. When that happens, choreographer and audience have the opportunity to gain deeper insight into both the biblical narrative and themselves. When a prophetic dance offends us, we are suddenly in the role of the kings of Israel in relation to the prophets. We become better able to understand how David felt when justly accused by Nathan of stealing another man's wife. No one likes having weaknesses exposed and favorite idols broken. But one of the basic assumptions made by people who hold biblical faiths is that no one—neither community nor prophet—is perfect.

However, if *Madre Tierra, Madre Lucha* were presented to a group of Salvadoran or Guatemalan refugees, it would probably be seen as a priestly dance: as a work lifting up and affirming the community's decisions and experience. This is the priestly function. When a dance affirms a community's past and present, drawing actions and events together into a statement that becomes to some degree symbolic of that group's hopes and self-image, it is playing a priestly role. Two theatrical examples of dances that do this for Americans are Agnes de Mille's *Rodeo* and Martha Graham's *Appalachian Spring*, both of which present affirming images of our frontier past. In the Body and Soul repertoire, three dances that have played this role are *Mary Alice's Magnificat*, a nonnarrative piece called *Sacred Harp Suite*, and *Sadie and Abe*, Phil Porter and Cynthia Winton-Henry's American frontier retelling of the biblical Sarah and Abraham story. American Christian congregations—especially Protestants, because of their more or less common musical heritage—usually perceive these dances as affirming a shared religious past. In the case of the first two, this perception is partly the result of the music: gospel hymns for the first, and early American Shape Note music for the second. The third dance resets a familiar religious story in our western pioneer cultural mythology, thus creating a priestly image that affirms two pasts: national and biblical.

It is interesting to notice that in the biblical narrative, the priestly role is especially important when a group is forging its identity and struggling to become established. The prophet becomes necessary after a person or group has gained power and feels secure in its possession. The assumption seems to be that while those trying to build something new need to be encouraged, the powerful need and ought to be challenged—in itself a challenging statement for the artist working in the contemporary American church.

Another important implication of accepting these two roles is that the dancer acknowledges the necessity of looking outside the self for dance ideas. Recent religious dance has often been the visualization of personal piety and self-discovery. It has been largely a dance of feeling. The dancer who responds to the biblical priest/prophet model learns to expand this approach, respecting form and craft as well as feeling, and finding promising dance material in issues and ideas as well as interior experiences. Creativity, of course, like the Spirit, "blows where it will," and no artist worth his or her salt creates simply to specification. The most closely defined commission, successfully carried out, is at some level unaccountable and unforeseen.

Nevertheless, both art and revelation are contextual. For example, as the churches become more genuinely inclusive of women in positions of leadership, it is important that art in the church reflect and comment on this growth. This means that we need to see men presenting exuberant dances of feeling, because, in our culture, exuberant expressiveness has been largely denied to men. At the same time, we need to see woman creating and performing work about issues and ideas, since rational and analytic power have been largely denied to women. As more women become leaders of congregations, the priestly and prophetic roles of *both* male and female artists carry expanded potential for ministry.

Today, a woman priest or pastor is, because of her ordination, her official leadership role in the community, and her liturgical function, simultaneously a priestly and a prophetic figure in all her actions. In parishes whose minister is a woman, the congregation is already grappling, joyously or otherwise, with the prophetic dimension of being the church. In such a situation, weighted on the prophetic side, the presentation of priestly work can be especially helpful. That is to say, such a parish may have a particular need to see dances affirming the community's struggles and joys, its past, its accomplishments and strengths. Taking care to include the priestly dimension of the arts can help a congregation to maintain a healthy and reassuring balance during a time of growth and new experience. Providing reassurance in this way enables people to remain more securely open to change.

Regardless of their particular situation, dancers and congregation usually begin with a natural leaning toward either the priestly or the prophetic role, and this leaning is often related to whether the performing arts are seen as windows or mirrors. These are two very different ways of understanding how the performing arts work within a community. When dance is understood primarily as window, its role resembles the role of art in the ancient Greek world, with its philosophy of ideal forms. These ideal forms were thought to be perceived in and through the physical world, though not perfectly. Religion and art allowed people to glimpse those perfect forms, and reminded them of the importance of imitating them individually and socially. When dance is understood in this way, attention is focused on the necessity of becoming more like particular ideals. A dance becomes a symbol of the distant ideal, and the performer becomes a link between seen and unseen, playing a mediating role.

When dance is understood as mirror, the focus is less on ideals and more on the community as it exists here and now. This attitude recalls the biblical focus on the community in a given time and place as the setting for revelation, representing not what ought to be, but what is. Not that what is is flawless, but that what is is where God is to be found and decisions are to be made. The performer and the performance become a metaphor for the community, saying in effect, "This is who we are. What does it mean? What shall we do about it?"

Each of these different ways of going about art in the church can be both priestly and prophetic. Each suggests four tasks for the artist. The first is simply for the performer to be conscious of these two different and theologically based conceptions of his or her art, and to balance the natural leaning toward a symbolic/window or a metaphoric/mirror way of working by making sure that, whichever is primary, *both* the priestly and the prophetic roles are reflected within the artist's self-understanding and repertoire. The second is to remember that it is context that determines whether something is priestly or prophetic. The third is to understand that congregations will experience both roles as helpful ministry at different points in their life together. And the fourth is to discern when each role is needed.

Whichever basic position a performer takes about the role of dance in the church—dance as window or dance as mirror—he or she sets up a delicately balanced relationship with the congregation as the roles of priest and prophet are played. On the one hand, the performer must respect the corporate identity and task of the congregation. On the other, the congregation must respect the individual vision and voice of the artist. This obligation of the congregation on behalf of the performer becomes more complicated when he or she is a member of the congregation and therefore part of its corporate identity. In order for this relationship to work, performer and congregation need to support and appreciate each other's gifts, agreeing that the church is not a showcase for either art or convention, but a place of dialogue among people in search of God and meaning.

When might a dancer play the priestly role? Examples from my own experience include performances at weddings, at funerals, for patients in a convalescent hospital, for an ecumenical congregation at a Thanksgiving service, and at the opening of a peace conference. In the first three situations, I danced *Mary Alice's Magnificat,* which, as the story of my grandmother's life, served to focus the life events of the communities involved. For the bride and groom and wedding guests, the dance was a romantic and joyous statement about relationship in the context of faith. As part of the funeral of a woman in her eighties, the dance affirmed a long life centered on family and service to others, and celebrated a new member of the communion of saints. In much the same way, it affirmed life and age and pointed toward being with God after death for the convalescent hospital audience. One patient told her nurse, "That's the most important thing I've ever seen." I think she meant that she saw herself in the dance, and felt the pieces of her life drawn together and blessed.

At the Thanksgiving service, where the other performers included a Salvation Army band and a gospel choir, I performed a piece called *Breath Given to Clay,* about being filled with God's breath and moved by the Spirit. The dance was a nonnarrative kinetic offering that helped draw a diverse congregation together by focusing attention not on what we believed in common (which was probably very little), but on what we experienced in common: bodies, minds, and spirits with which to respond to God.

At a Berkeley peace conference, Body and Soul performed *Basic Training,* by Phil Porter. *Basic Training,* which presents militarism and its inevitable result, war, is usually perceived by audiences and considered by the company as a more or less prophetic dance. But when done for a gathering of peace activists, it played a priestly role by affirming the group's already-made decision that militarism and war are to be opposed.

When dance plays a prophetic role, humor is often part of the result. I have come to believe that one of the most important things the arts can do for the church is to bring the gifts of humor and a loving irreverence to theological reflection and the life of the community. *3-in-1-and-1-in-3*, our company's piece about the Trinity, has provided a humorous look at theological language for many audiences. One of these was the Earl Lectures audience in Berkeley in 1981, when well-known German theologian Jürgen Moltmann was the lecturer. Just before Dr. Moltmann spoke on the Trinity, the company presented *3-in-1*, surprising the audience not a little with this hilarious romp through the theological enterprise. Dr. Moltmann in turn surprised the dancers. He began his talk by saying that, since the company had in essence given his lecture for him, he would just add a few *foot*notes!

A Merry Meeting, about the pregnant Mary and Elizabeth, also plays a prophetic role in relation to issues of masculine and feminine identity. As has been said, being encouraged to reflect on *A Merry Meeting* has given some men new access to feminine imagery and its ability to illumine and enrich their own psychological and spiritual journeys. For both women and men struggling with our culture's confusing messages about parenthood, the dancers' flaunting and reveling in being with child comes as a surprise—and sometimes as a delight!

There is at least one situation in which the dancer must be both prophet and priest at the same time: when he or she is introducing dance into a congregation. Whether this takes place in a lecture-demonstration, workshop, or worship service, the dancer must both challenge and reassure. If the dancer does *too* much reassuring through the content and style of what is performed, dance is likely to be perceived as irrelevant and boring, and the congregation will come away still not knowing that dance is a powerful communicative form that can do things words cannot. If the dancer is only challenging, the congregation may withdraw in confusion, rejecting dance as difficult and inappropriate.

I have found that the easiest way to be reassuring and authoritative priest as well as challenging prophet in this situation is to present a conceptually strong and kinetically lively dance, and to make at some point in the event, before the dance begins, a verbal doorway through which the audience may enter into the performance. This is not the same thing as trying to "explain" a dance, because no dance worth performing can be reduced to a verbal equivalent. Nor is it the same thing as an "apology" for dance, though some historical background may be helpful for a congregation or audience. Instead, it is a verbal framework that gives the watchers some basic artistic and theological ground to stand on as they encounter the work. For example, it is very helpful to talk about what kinesthetic identification is and how it works, and to remind the audience of the variety of ways, nonverbal and verbal, in which we gather information and experience in our daily lives. First-time watchers also need to hear that dance is not a sign language or pantomime in which a verbal equivalent can be found for the movements.

When some clues about the nature of the artform are given, dance is made accessible not only to those already familiar with it, and to those ready to reach out intuitively for new experience, but also to those accustomed to value only the verbal, and to those who may be shy about responding to new things. If priestly care is taken to include all of these people in an initial experience with dance, then the way is prepared for dance to play both the prophetic and the priestly roles as an artform respected by the whole community. But it must be stressed that this approach presupposes that the dance presented to first-time watchers is artistically sound, avoiding neither physical exuberance nor intellectual challenge in a mistaken attempt to ease the congregation's first encounter. Timid dance, often defended on the basis of "what the congregation will think," is a disservice to all involved.

If dance is to play a role in the church's life comparable to that which music already plays, it is important, when dance is presented in worship, *not* to create a service that is "about" dance. The point rather is to create dance that kinetically illumines a scripture reading, a theological or social issue, or a liturgical moment that would be part of the normal worship experience whether or not dance were present. Otherwise, dance remains an occasional and special interest.

All of this discussion about the qualifications and roles of the performer refers mostly to the time before and after performance. But what happens to and for the dancer in the performance space? What are we really seeing when we see a dancer performing? First of all, we are seeing someone whose presence represents an enormous investment of time and money; he or she has probably spent thousands of dollars and hours learning to dance. An hour-and-a-half class now costs about seven dollars, and class is, for many dancers, an almost daily event for as long as the dancer's performing career lasts. The cost of training often includes college, conservatory, or graduate school tuition in a dance program. In addition, there are the costs of special summer courses and workshops, dance clothes, costumes, tapes, props, and the hours of creative and rehearsal time, for which many dancers, especially in the church, are not paid.

In the days and weeks before performance, the dancer has been especially wary of injury—always a threat. Cynthia Winton-Henry of Body and Soul told me about a narrow escape, a few days before a major company performance, from what would have been a catastrophic car accident. As the car in which she was riding dodged the oncoming car, she found herself thinking, "I can't die now. Judith would *kill* me!" Injury also looms as a potential financial disaster. It is a sad comment on the financial difficulty of dancers' lives that many— perhaps most—of those whose bodies are their instruments do not have health insurance because they cannot afford it.

If the performance includes live music, the musicians and the dancer have probably not had adequate rehearsal time together, for financial and other reasons. Each hopes that the other will prove to be a reliable partner, able to cope professionally with whatever happens during the piece. If the sound is taped, the dancer hopes that the sound technician has paid attention to the cues, and that the sound equipment is in good working order.

The dancer also hopes that there will be no surprises in the previously agreed upon arrangements of the dancing space. In spite of our best efforts to communicate about space needs, these surprises come in a never-ending variety to dancers working in churches. I have found a full orchestra occupying all of the supposed dancing area except for a few feet off to one side; a ten-foot decorated Christmas tree in the middle of the chancel and banks of poinsettias on the steps; a rotund and slow-moving bishop who mistook his liturgical cue and turned a solo into a duet; and an emotionally troubled person who disrobed before the altar as the astonished dance company waited in the chancel for its musical cue—and as the congregation concluded that the disrobing individual must be one of the dancers!

These external eventualities safely negotiated, what goes on inside the dancer during a dance? First of all, the physical and mental effort to execute the moves of the dance as precisely and beautifully as possible, neither rushing, hesitating, blurring, nor forgetting. Then the effort to use the space well, so that particular sequences happen in particular places; the dancer must intentionally use the space available, trying not to seem cramped in a small space or lost in a large one. The edge of the stage or the furniture of the chancel must be kept in awareness. One's own internal workings—growling stomach or running nose—must be coped with. An emotional and kinetic contact must be established and maintained with the audience, so that the dance is a journey on which they go rather than a picture at which they gaze. If the dance is a group piece, a strong sense of responsiveness and working together must be maintained in relation to the other dancers. Mistakes, including one's own, those of other dancers, and those of musicians and sound and light technicians, have to be noticed and absorbed into the flow of the performance, so that the audience does not know a mistake has been made.

At a studio performance of Charles Weidman's *Brahms*

Waltzes, danced by Carol Geneve and Frank Shawl, the music tape broke. Without missing a step, Geneve said, "Shall we speak it, then? Rise . . . and fall . . . now we turn and slide. . . . " In perfect cadence and with complete aplomb the performers finished the dance, while those in the audience who, like me, had not seen the piece before, marveled at Weidman's having thought of such a clever and effective use of the dancer's voice as accompaniment for the movement.

When there is live music, a visual and auditory relationship has to be maintained between dancer and musician throughout the performance. (Though not always possible, live music is the first choice in worship settings. Taped music in worship, inevitably contrasting with the warm aliveness of voices and instruments, can cast a spell of artificiality and remoteness.) The relationship between dancer and musician is especially crucial in improvisation, in which the entire performance is built on a flexible, responsive, and secure relationship between sound and movement, created in the moment.

During all of the above, the dancer is also often peripherally aware of other events in the space—people coughing or whispering, children crying; is perhaps silently counting throughout a new piece in order not to lose the place in the music; is dealing with the vagaries of costumes and props; is keeping track of facial expression; and is remembering to breathe correctly and evenly.

These lists are enough to make us wonder about the frequent assertion that, while dancing in worship, a dancer is or ought to be praying. There is certainly enough to pray about, but that is not usually what is meant! I have found that two quite different concerns can prompt this statement. One is the speaker's discomfort with the idea of performance. If we cannot admit performance as a valid activity in worship, we have to conceive of the dancer as doing something else while we watch; and so we say that the dancer is not performing but praying. This perspective tends to privatize dance in the setting in which, of all others, dance ought to intend and achieve a strong relationship with the watching community. It also denies the rich potential of dance as performing art for the church, limiting the congregation's understanding of what they are seeing, and the artist's potential offerings to the community.

But a valid insight about how different traditions regard worship can also lead to the assertion that the dancer is praying. In those churches in which the eucharist is seen as the center of worship, corporate thanksgiving is emphasized, and the dancer is often seen as part of that emphasis. In contrast, traditions that place preaching at the center of worship most often regard the dancer as part of the business of proclamation.

Whatever liturgical and theological tradition the performer represents, he or she can become an important presence in the community—challenging and affirming it, deepening its engagement with issues and the surrounding culture, and expanding its understanding of religious leadership—if the fluid roles of priest and prophet are embraced and sensitively explored.

SUMMARY

Among those interested in the arts in the church, there has been lively discussion about whether the dancer or musician may be called a performer within a religious context. Underlying some of this questioning is a good deal of misunderstanding about what it means to perform, as well as uneasiness about the level of expertise demanded of the artist in the church.

But if we understand both amateur and professional, the simply competent and the supremely talented, as selflessly serving a craft at different levels of commitment and ability in order to communicate, much of the confusion is resolved. The amateur is one who does something for the love of doing it; loving something dictates making the effort to do it well. The professional is one who does something for the love of it, and also with the intention of earning a living from it. Both must bring disciplined realism to their work.

Part of this discipline and realism is the acceptance of the biblical roles of priest and prophet. Whether the artist draws largely on already composed music or dance, or creates new pieces, both the musician and the dancer share the calling to be for their communities sometimes priest and sometimes prophet. Dance in the church has a greater freedom to explore its prophetic role than does music, because it has a shorter history and therefore less tradition. Music in the church, with its long and rich history, demonstrates the capabilities inherent in a historically self-aware artform. Musicians and dancers need to learn from each other in these areas.

The priestly artist reminds us who we are and where we have come from. He or she affirms our past and offers us the firm ground of tradition on which to stand. As prophet, the artist challenges us with who we were created to be, asks us where we are going, and calls us into the future. The link between priest and prophet is a deep commitment to the community's tradition. The priest reassures us that we do indeed stand within it, and the prophet insists that we measure ourselves against it and refrain from idolizing it.

The priestly and prophetic roles of the performer are most clearly identified, and their ministry most fully experienced, in the context of the concerns and issues facing particular communities. An obvious contemporary context for defining these roles is to be found in the new opportunities and challenges created by the growing number of women who are religious leaders. As the church deepens its insight and commitment in this area, we need to see prophetic work that calls us out of our sexist and exclusive ways of understanding the world, and we also need to see priestly work that reassures us that our essential community identity and traditions are holding firm through this time of change. In this and other contexts, the full range and power of music and dance to nurture and enable become available to the church when its artists take upon themselves the yoke of this double role.

Phil Porter in his We'll Find Time. *Photo: Kingmond Young*

Chapter 5

Art as Pentecost

DANCE: BRINGER OF VISION

The story of Pentecost, told in the second chapter of Acts, is a story of people who cannot understand each other suddenly hearing a voice from home out of the mouth of each outlandish stranger. It is a fitting festival of the church, committed as it is to bringing faith out of bafflement. When we speak of art as pentecost, we acknowledge that dance, music, and all the arts can be bringers of vision to ordinary contemporary people.

As the story goes, the onlookers thought the disciples were drunk, behaving inappropriately for disciples. Ever since, the church has tended to confuse the surprises of the spirit with inappropriateness. The arts, especially the performing arts, and most especially dance, have often been thought inappropriate because they are inextricably bound up with play.

Embracing dance means embracing play and surprise. Pentecost affirms that human control and limitation are not the final word about anything. Accepting and supporting the arts and artists underlines this kind of volatile theology, and churches are often understandably hesitant. It takes humility for a person or an institution to open the door to the unexpected. But once the door is open, the party can begin!

To say that dance as a performing art affirms that human control and limitation are not the final word about reality is, of course, a paradox. As we have seen, the dancer's technique, choreography, and performance cannot happen without discipline and control; a profound acknowledgment and affirmation

95

of limitation is always necessary in order to create. The paradox is that out of this disciplined realism can rise a soaring vision. Taut muscles, a supple back, the sudden bursting of a body through space can, for a moment, peel back a corner of the ordinary and let the mystery through.

Because of their power to do this for us, the arts remind us how modest our hopes are and how dim our normal vision is. When I walked into visual artist Tony Duquette's Los Angeles exhibit, "Our Lady Queen of the Angels," I was consumed with the thought—or the prayer—"I hope it's true. Let it be true." With wire, bone, fabric, feathers, light, wind, and sound, the artist dredged up in me the ancient hope. Uriel, Gabriel, Michael, Rafael. "There are four angels at my head," I prayed every night in childhood, and again standing in the midst of Duquette's vision.

One cause of the extravagant, often irrelevant-seeming things artists do is that they get so easily drunk on reality and its implications. Part of their gift is to be able to grab the rest of us by the lapels and shout—or whisper—"look, listen, marvel!"—so that suddenly, through the chaos, we hear a voice from home. There has been much discussion of whether those who do this for us in church settings should be Christian, to the exclusion of others. The truth is that we need all the help we can get in trying to know God and each other, and that we can be thankful for *whoever*, as J. R. R. Tolkien put it, lets a gleam come through the web of the world. We have been warned that the wind of the Spirit blows where it will.

However, the dancer who wants to work primarily in the church will probably (though not necessarily) be a Christian and will certainly need theological expertise, because a career in dance and religion is interdisciplinary. When hiring a choreographer, though, the church will do well to make the first criterion the ability to make exciting and excellent dance, rather than a particular theological point of view.

Behind the question of whether the dancer or choreographer working in the church ought to be a Christian is a question about intentions versus acts. In some circles, the church has tended to praise (or at least to refrain from criticizing) most art created with a religious intention. Charitable though this attitude may be, it does not reflect a biblical theology. In the Bible, the important thing is the act of the person in question, not his or her feelings or intentions. What matters is the thing done. Because a dance is an act, it should be judged as an effective or ineffective act—judged on the terms of dance criticism as a dance, and judged by what happens to and for its watchers while it is going on and after it is over. If people are enlivened as givers of thanks for beauty, affirmed as capable decision makers, challenged to love, helped to laugh, moved to concern for their neighbor, then that dance probably has a place in the church, whatever the choreographer or dancer happens to believe about the mystery of life.

If dance brings us to new insight, it does so partly by means of play. The dance company Pilobolus has in its repertoire a piece in which dancers, using a special floor surface, slide at breakneck speed on back, side, and belly from one side of the stage to the other. The audience is thrilled; muscle memories of rolling down hills, sliding down banisters, ice skating, and sliding into home base are revived. Today many men and women are exercise- and fitness-conscious. But we often run and work out in grim pursuit of something: health, beauty, youth, prowess. Adults rarely indulge (or at least rarely admit to indulging) in exuberant physicality for the sheer purposeless fun of it. Scores of grownups run; very few climb trees. Part of the business of dance in the church is to restore our sense of physical play and physical joyousness.

Issues of sensuality and sexuality are, of course, immediately raised. For adults of all ages, enjoying the body's possibilities usually implies sexuality. Because dance is the artform of the body, it is closely connected to sexuality and easily suggests it. This is one reason the church has sometimes been officially wary of dance. The attempt to avoid this "threat" of sexuality also accounts for the blandness and kinetically impractical costuming of some contemporary church dance. Dance can nurture us spiritually, but it is a contradiction in terms to try to make dances that are more spiritual than physical. Trying

97

to create a dance that is somehow more spiritual than physical is not unlike trying to create music that is more inaudible than audible. If transcendence and meaning are to shine through dance, they can do so *only* through intense physicality. It is the physical world that is the theater of revelation, the physical world that leads us to spirituality. Instead of trying to hide the male or female dancing body under bloodless gesture and sexless drapery, we can approach dance as an opportunity for the whole congregation to regain a more spacious sense of physical enjoyment in which sexuality is one of many bodily dimensions.

The more closely men and women work together in the church, the farther each goes from stereotyped roles in activities and leadership, the more essential it is that we feel at home with and in our sexuality. Otherwise we will trip over it, apologize for it, hide behind it, manipulate with it. Dancers, whose strong, visible bodies are their only instruments, are perhaps the best equipped among artists to help the body-shy and physically inarticulate come to terms with their physicality.

Imagine that an adult education group has decided to do a study of six weeks or so exploring the Christian attitude to the body. They decide to consider, among other things, the biblical attitude toward the physical world, various Christian understandings of sexuality, the vein of asceticism that runs through Christianity, the self-forgetfulness that is part of grace, and the perhaps differing attitudes of men and women toward play. The course has three leaders: one with the necessary theological and psychological expertise, and two dancers—a woman and a man accustomed to performing together and to teaching. As part of each class meeting, the dancers lead movement sessions for the group, focusing on flexibility, physical freedom, and contact improvisation. These are not technical dance classes, but movement sessions, in which reasonably fit adults of all ages can take part. After each period of time spent with movement, the three leaders encourage discussion and reflection in response to the movement experiences and in relation to the verbal content of the course. At two or three sessions, the dancers present several duets, followed by discussion about partnering in dance, its relation to attitudes toward the body, its place in dance in the church, and the responses of class members as they watch the partnering.

Partnering, the physical contact of one dancer with another by which one helps the other to perform particular movements, is rarely seen in worship or in other church contexts. It has an important role to pay, however. Partnering speaks to us of love, support, trust, risk, and commitment. It offers imagery that affirms our daily relationships. As a statement that we ultimately yield ourselves to relationship or we don't, partnering can be extraordinarily beautiful as well as emotionally moving. It is also a theologically appropriate challenge to an unspoken feeling on the part of many Christians that sexuality and sensuality have little or no visible place in the church.

In their duet called *Point of Contact,* Robert Yohn and Kristin Peterson explore the nuances and risks of trusting oneself to another. The dance, performed in both theatrical and religious settings, can also be seen, by implication and context, as a meditation on the delight and risk of trusting oneself to God's love. The sudden and apparently dangerous lifts, the tender moments of repose in balance, the dizzy swooping through space take the audience on a physical journey of fear, risk, and surprise. Whether we respond primarily to the human or the divine metaphor contained in this dance, we are obliged to admit to ourselves that trusting another is not only a decision, but a series of acts.

Of course, one difficulty with partnering is that usually the stronger person who does the lifting is the man, while the smaller person who is lifted is the woman. To avoid undue underscoring of sexist assumptions about women, men, and God, dancers must continue to explore and create partnering in which the woman supports the man, and in which two men or two women work together, as well as the more traditional partnering in which the man supports and the woman is supported.

Most of us are familiar with the worldview in which "religious" things are thought of as "higher," somehow having to do with the head, while "worldly" things are thought of as "lower," somehow having to do with the pelvis. A leftover from ancient—and not so ancient—heresies, this viewpoint reflects the tendency to see spirituality as good and physicality as evil. Dance that involves partnering can be a catalyst for challenging these assumptions, helping the congregation to look again at the oddly braided skein of physical and sexual imagery that runs through Christianity. This rich tangle includes the poetry of St. John of the Cross, the Song of Songs, the imagery of Christ as bridegroom—and even sentimental hymns such as "In the Garden." The physicality of dance opens doorways into an understanding and appreciation of this imagery.

As women who are pastors, priests, theologians, and chaplains suggest new visions of the church, we are discovering that their voices tell us not only about ourselves and our contemporary situation; they also illumine parts of our tradition, such as the intense sensuality of some mystics, that have seemed anomalous to many Christians. If we can include sexuality and sensuality in our experience of faith, we will be able to take advantage of the new opportunity the contemporary feminist presence gives us to see our entire tradition with new eyes. Unacknowledged confusion in clergy and congregation about the relation of sexuality and sensuality, about the varieties of sexuality, about appropriate professional and pastoral relationships between women and men and between people of the same sex, and about the power and possibility offered by one's own inner masculine and feminine traits: all of this confusion cries out to the church to help us address our sexuality in ways that are intuitive, holistic, and open-ended. Otherwise, we will miss the theological and spiritual grace our new inclusiveness offers. Because it is the artform of the body, dance can be a powerful—and humorous—way to begin to work with the relationships among sexuality, sensuality, and faith.

Biblical study is another area in which dance can offer new understanding. Using performance dance in Bible study develops our capacity to let one kind of thing illumine a different kind of thing. Seeing relationships between unlike things come more naturally to some people than to others; but we can all profit from it, because it enlarges our mental categories and loosens their hold. Categories are like fences: sometimes useful for sorting things out, sometimes obstacles keeping us from getting where we want to go. When dance is invited into the process of Bible study, the goal is for a dance to illumine a biblical passage and for the passage to illumine the dance.

This interplay works best when the dance is not a close visual interpretation or acting out of the passage, but when the choreographer has used the passage as a jumping-off point for a kinetic statement. When this is done, the dance carries us into a nonlinear, nonverbal dimension in which we can see new combinations of ideas and images. We then return to the biblical passage with eyes open, ears washed out, muscles working. Our relationship to the passage has expanded from our verbal head into our moving body. If the dance has done its job, it has helped us examine our preconceptions about this passage in particular and maybe about the Bible in general.

We are all familiar with the way the sudden conjunction of unlike things tells us something new. That is the way both poetry and jokes work. Phil Porter of Body and Soul uses the sudden meeting of unlike with unlike in a joke as the beginning point of a solo dance called *We'll Find Time*. He begins the piece by telling a joke: A man driving down a country road looked over to see a farmer standing under an apple tree, holding a pig in his arms while the pig ate apples off the tree. The man pulled over in disbelief and asked, "What are you doing?" "Feedin' the pigs," the farmer replied. "But wouldn't it be easier—and save a lot of time, too—if you just knocked the apples off the tree and let the pig eat them off the ground?" "Well," said the farmer, "I s'pose it would. But what's time to a pig?"

Feelings and thoughts jump over the fences of our categories, creating a new landscape of meaning for us. Bible study built on this concept might be explored in the following way. The teacher of the course first locates a choreographer or company with perhaps four dances based on or loosely related to biblical stories; he or she then plans an eight-week study, using those four passages. At alternate sessions, the dancers present a dance, which is integrated into the session in various ways. Two sessions are spent on each story, one with dance as a centerpiece, the other using the more traditional methods of reflection. In the four sessions using dance, the sequence varies. Sometimes the dance is presented first, followed by a reading or telling of the story, then discussion, with the dance presented again at the end of the class time. At another session, the passage might be read, the dance presented, time given for silent reflection on what has been heard and seen, and finally a guided meditation offered, drawing on material from the passage and images from the dance. Another possibility is that, after listening to the passage, the class is divided into small groups or pairs to talk about their thoughts and associations as they listened; then the dance is presented, and the class again divides into groups to talk about their thoughts and associations as they watched. The whole group reassembles toward the end of the session to discuss differences in and relationships between their responses to the passage as read and to the dance. The dancers are involved as class participants in the sessions at which they dance.

It is important to notice that in this scenario the teacher's choice of passages is based on dances that are readily available. If the passages are chosen first, dances that relate to them will probably have to be commissioned by the church. Commissioning dance, though a costly and time-consuming undertaking, can be a very exciting and rewarding venture for both congregation and choreographer. Its steps will be discussed later in this chapter.

Dance is most effective as a vision-bringer in worship when it is also used as part of education. For many reasons, worship can be the most difficult setting into which to introduce dance. It is often the time in the church week most hedged about with prescriptions and proscriptions. It is also sometimes the place where people feel most personally restrained. From childhood, and especially in some styles of worship, we learn to smother our physicality in the sanctuary: sit still, don't talk, don't laugh, don't sing too loudly. While some of these rules may be necessary some of the time, it is not immediately apparent to many people why Psalm 150's injunction to "praise God with timbrel and dance" should suddenly take precedence over this life-long learning. But if dance is already being used in the church's program of adult education, both as performance and as participatory event, some in the congregation will have begun to understand both the artform and its relevance for the church.

As we saw in Chapter 4, dance can be both prayer and proclamation in worship. If proclamation is emphasized, dance is most likely to be found in relationship to scripture and sermon. Both choreographed pieces and improvisation can be used. If a choreographed or "set" piece is used, perhaps in relation to one of the scripture readings, a worship order that allows for the repetition of the dance is helpful. Dance, especially modern dance, is an unfamiliar artform for many people. Even those accustomed to looking at dance appreciate seeing a piece more than once in order to see into it. One possible order is to have the scripture read, the dance presented, a shorter-than-usual sermon preached, and then the dance repeated in the remaining sermon time. This order presupposes that the preacher will attend at least one rehearsal of the dance as an integral part of his or her sermon preparation, so that dance, sermon, and scripture are tightly related in terms of idea. The dance should probably not be longer than three or four minutes, and the sermon not longer than ten minutes.

The presentation of set pieces in worship, while probably offering the richest experience of dance to a congregation, can be very difficult for everyone concerned because of space limitations. Body and Soul, after several years of unscrewing pews and moving chancel furniture, has turned partly to improvisation in the worship setting as a way to solve this problem. Improvisation is practical in that the dancers can make spontaneous use of whatever possibilities and limitations the space offers. As a form, it also raises interesting theological and personal questions for the watchers, since all our relationships, including our relationship with God, take place in the midst of our not knowing for sure what will happen next. Of course we make, individually and corporately, fairly predictable structures for our lives: job, family, liturgy. But part of the purpose of those structures is to provide a secure place to stand while we open the door to the unknown. The church sometimes fosters a false sense of security through a worship format that barely acknowledges the unexpected. Being a structure for the incorporation of the unforeseen, improvisation affirms that when we lift a foot from now and put it down in then, we step into the unknown and must respond to it out of what we know. The theological heart of improvisation is the relation of trust and choice: we trust that, out of our experience with the familiar, we will know what to do in the face of something new. We trust that we *will* respond to God, others, and ourselves; and we *choose* a way, sometimes an untried way, in which to respond. Improvisation and ethics are unlikely but interesting cousins.

When improvisation is used, there are several important guidelines to follow. First, improvisation as performance is only for experienced improvisers with a solid technical background. The improvising dancer must have a secure technical vocabulary from which to draw movement ideas, if the dancing is to be worth watching. He or she must also be secure as a performer, in order to be able to focus on the necessity of movement repetition, and of kinetic response to other dancers and musicians—all crucial aspects of improvisation. Second, the congregation needs to *know* that they are seeing improvisation. Done by skilled performers, this kind of dance can be at first glance indistinguishable from a set piece. When the audience is told that the dancers and the musicians will be improvising, they participate in the excitement of not knowing what is next, and in the delight of how wonderful the unplanned can be.

Usually when improvisation is used, it is important that *both* musicians and dancers be improvising. Otherwise, it is difficult to maintain a relational balance between the music and the dance. Paradoxically, improvisation involves rehearsal: the performers need to spend time together, understanding each other's styles, "jamming," and setting guidelines for the piece they will present. These planned limits usually include length, the nature of various sections, and transitional cues.

Improvisation can be used, as set pieces are, in relation to scripture and sermon. One possibility is scriptural improvisation in which several people from the congregation with strong speaking voices provide the sound. First of all, the scripture is read straight through in the usual way. Then the voices, from different locations in the sanctuary, begin to "play" with individual words and phrases from the passage. This play is verbally nonsequential, a small number of words is used, and large spaces of silence are left. The dancers join in, and a "conversation" develops, a jazzlike embroidery on the passage. This "commentary" leads directly into the sermon. A second section of the improvisation completes the sermon.

One little-explored possibility for dance in worship is the presentation of pieces based on historical Christian dance. Originally ritual movement for large groups, these dances (about which we know only a little) can be used as the basis for simple contemporary performance pieces. These might be a good choice for a developing dance group with modest technical skills. For example, one Ash Wednesday, a Catholic group used a reconstruction of the medieval Dance of Death, a dance-game in which a skeleton figure drags dancers out of a circle to "die" in the center of the ring. As worshipers arrived for the midday service, they had to walk past the dance, which was taking place in the courtyard. Only the performers were pounced on by Death, but passing close to the dance served as a fitting and physical entrance into the service. It was the costumed Death figure who, during the liturgy, put the ashes on the foreheads of the congregation, saying, "Dust thou art, to dust thou shalt return."

Another ancient dance that can be presented as a performance piece, particularly at the Easter Vigil, is the Labyrinth Dance, whose symbolism has to do with passing through death into life. The church may have inherited it from the Greeks, who used it in relation to the story of Theseus freeing the youths and maidens of Athens from the Minotaur's labyrinth. Many medieval cathedrals had mazes tiled into their floors for dancing through at Easter; one of the best examples, the maze at Chartres, can still be seen. A performance piece can be made that uses a Greek-style line weaving snakelike down the aisle, the leader carrying a candle. When the line reaches the open space at the front of the church, the pattern becomes a more complex and visible labyrinth, covering all of the chancel space as though the dancers were threading a maze. Flute and drum accompaniment, preferably in an uneven meter, possibly five or seven, is effective because of its strangeness. The dance finishes with the proclamation, "Christ is risen!" and the congregation's response, "He is risen indeed!"

When historical dances are taken as a base for contemporary pieces, bridges are built between contemporary performance dance in the church and dance as a very old, though largely lost, part of Christian ritual. Though it is helpful for people to know something of the history of church dance, it is usually better not to lean too heavily on either history or biblical evidence as justifying the contemporary use of dance. Occurrence in the past is not necessarily a good reason for use in the present. A stronger case can be made for dance in the church by using the historical and biblical evidence as a foundation on which to build a contemporary theology of dance and the body.

If dance is to be a pentecost experience for a church community in education and worship, as proclamation and prayer, time and effort will be needed to find the best possible dance. There are several options for the congregation looking for dance. First, there may be a professional dancer or choreographer within the congregation who would like to work in the church setting. It is possible that such a person may want to offer his or her services free of charge. But it needs to be remembered that most dancers live financially precarious lives, working on a season or freelance basis. The congregation should assume that a sizable fee/honorarium will be paid and budget accordingly. A fee scale can be arrived at by discussing current professional fees with the choreographer in question and with other members of the dance community. This means planning ahead, so that when a dancer is approached, the money to support the work is already in the budget. (The well-intentioned but difficult situation in which a dancer is approached about an exciting project, only to be told that it can't be done until the money is somehow found for it, should be avoided. This kind of approach can put subtle pressure on the already financially struggling dancer to work for less than he or she feels is necessary.)

There may, of course, be an in-house dance group giving its dancing as a gift to the congregation on an ongoing basis, in which case members would not expect to be paid for performance in their home church. However, such a group and its director should be included in the church budget on the same basis as the choir and its director, depending on the frequency of the dancers' performances or other contributions.

A congregation looking for dance might consider forming a small committee and sending it out into the community to attend dance concerts. This is somewhat more feasible for congregations in urban areas, but today many smaller towns have at least one dance company; some have both a ballet and a modern company. The small-town ballet is often made up of well-trained young people at the apprentice level who hope to be professional dancers. College dance departments sometimes include modern dance companies. Promising young dancers and experienced directors are available through many of these groups; most would appreciate the opportunity to try a new project.

When the committee sees work it likes, it approaches the choreographer or company in question to discuss inviting them to present that or other work in relation to some aspect of the church's life, such as adult education or worship. The committee will probably find that, while some artists may not want to work in the religious setting, many will be intrigued by the possibility, and some will already have considerable experience working in churches, synagogues, or other religious communities. Key issues to settle between committee and dancers are money, timetable, the context in which the dance will be seen, and space considerations.

Especially important to discuss is the size of the dancing

107

space and the nature of the floor on which the dancers will perform. Stone and concrete, whether carpeted or not, dictate either minimal jumping or no jumping at all, in order to avoid injury to the dancers. A wooden floor (not laid directly over stone or concrete) or a portable dance surface (which can be rented in many towns and cities) is essential if much jumping is to be done.

There are several other space considerations that may seem obvious but that, as many dancers working in churches have learned, often do need mentioning and explaining. One of these is ceiling height. Dancers need a high-ceilinged space. This is rarely a problem in worship spaces or in social halls, but can be in other church rooms. Leaping dancers can put their hands through light fixtures, and dancers being lifted can hit their heads in a normal room with an eight-foot ceiling. Another thing to remember is that closer is not better for the audience looking at dance, especially in a small space. In a social hall or gym or worship space, the watchers need to be far enough away from the dance to see its design as a whole. If they are too close, they will see only foreshortened individual dancers, and they may even be uneasy about the swirling activity going on almost in their laps.

Measurements of the available dancing space—not including seating area—are essential for the choreographer and performers. If the space is surrounded by walls of any kind, such as the sides of choir stalls, or is bounded by sheer edges, such as steps, the dancing space is automatically lessened by about a foot in each direction, since the extreme edges of such space are mostly unusable for movement. Most concert pieces are made for an open, level performing area measuring at least twenty by thirty feet. Many are made for far larger spaces. A choreographer can create for almost *any* space, whatever its floor surface and size, but usually only a commissioned work (or an improvisation) will fit into the six-by-eight-foot rectangle that so often turns out to be the reality behind someone's blithe assurance that "yes, we have a nice big chancel!" It is not that the speaker has set out to deceive the unwary dancer. It is simply that dance takes far more space than anything else that goes on in most churches, and most churches have not yet had enough experience with dance and dancers to realize what dance needs.

The other space problem for dancers that very often goes unmentioned is the single steps or level changes so beloved of church architects when it comes to designing chancels. For the dancer, a rectangle twenty feet deep and thirty feet wide, with a single step up at its midpoint, is generally usable only as two ten-by-thirty-foot rectangles—unless, of course, a piece is being created especially for that space, in which case the level change can become an asset to the choreographer. But if a company is trying to put a set piece normally performed on one flat level into such a space, the problems they face are not only difficult but dangerous. A single step up or down is hardly noticed by a sedately walking celebrant. But to a dancer performing complex footwork or big jumps, it can seem roughly equivalent to the Grand Canyon. (Improvisation lessens but does not do away with the potential danger. I write this with one leg in a cast, as a result of a torn muscle acquired by jumping down a small step during an improvisation in a cathedral.)

Finally, dancers need warmth. Muscles can tear because of cold. Body and Soul has shivered through rehearsals and performances in countless refrigeratorlike worship spaces. Perhaps the coldest was a small and very beautiful twelfth-century village church in England; the evening congregation at that November service appeared to be wearing every garment they owned, while we, in our California-weight costumes, were shaking so we could hardly move. Twelfth-century churches with eight hundred years of English damp in their fortresslike walls are almost impossible to heat. But in most situations involving dance, a little advance planning and some extra money in the heating budget will solve the problem.

Once a committee seeking dance for its congregation has found a choreographer, outlined a project, agreed on a budget, and taken care of space needs, a collaborative process is begun. The committee's job is to make the context and purpose of the event for which the dance is wanted as clear as possible, and then to be available for theological, liturgical, and other con-sultation. The choreographer's job is to produce a dance that, within agreed upon guidelines of time and theme, in some way illumines the event. Key words here are "in some way." An artist is commissioned to make a new and surprising thing; having made its needs and dreams clear, the committee should adopt a mostly hands-off attitude toward the specific shaping of the piece.

It is important for a church commissioning dance to re-member that it is often not productive to "assign" a piece of music along with a commission. My own experience is that this is often done, and that the music "assigned" is rarely either suitable for dance, or stimulating to me as a choreogra-pher. A given piece of music can be very beautiful and emo-tionally moving as part of worship, but not danceable. Or it may be beautiful, moving, and danceable—but not interesting to a particular choreographer. The most fruitful approach is either to let the choreographer choose the music, or to ask the choreographer and the church musician to collaborate on the choice. In any case, the choreographer should not have to "fight" the music throughout the choreographic process; the less experienced the choreographer, the more important this consideration becomes.

When a dance is commissioned, it is a good idea to build into the agreement and the budget the use of the same dance several times in different settings. The performance of a dance grows and deepens with repetition, as does the viewing. For example, the piece might be used at least twice in worship; once at an evening lecture-demonstration by the choreographer or company, in which the new dance can be seen in the context of other work by the same artist(s); as the program for a church family evening; in a children's lecture-demonstration in the church school; and for one of the church's special-interest groups, such as women, men, or youth depending on the nature of the dance. In this way, the dancers and choreographer have the satisfaction of seeing the piece live and grow, and the congre-gation has a chance to develop a relationship with the dance and the dancers, being moved by the dance in different ways as it is seen repeatedly in different situations.

Dance as pentecost is the invitation to learn a new language in which the Spirit can speak. It is a language of image and allusion, of masculine and feminine, of physicality and discipline. It can communicate many nuances of God-with-us that our usual languages of speech and print cannot communicate nearly so well. It is a bold language meant for joking, questioning, loving. One of the ancient languages of all religious people, it has returned to us as a contemporary language of the church. Broad comedy, prophetic fury, quiet prayer, strange vision, it offers us the gift of ourselves: re-membered, brought whole once again to the business of relationship, both human and divine.

I once made a dance for a Pentecost Sunday mass and named it after Richard Wilbur's poem "Love Calls Us to the Things of This World." The dance was built around the concept of nonsequitur—that is, something that doesn't follow logically from something else, which is another way to say surprise. Toward the middle of the piece, each dancer went to a member of the congregation, chosen on the spot and at random. The dancer confidentially put a hand on that person's shoulder and said, "You know, I really wasn't expecting this." Looking the dancer who had approached her straight in the eye, one woman, who seemed to be speaking for the whole church through the ages, replied in ringing tones, "Neither was I, young man!"

The dance ended with this litany:

DANCERS: From being so sure of the sequence that we never learn the dance—
CONGREGATION: Good Lord, deliver us.
DANCERS: From being so sure we know what the church looks like that we miss eucharist among us—
CONGREGATION: Good Lord, deliver us.
ALL: Come, Holy Spirit, and give us back our ancient love of surprises.

MUSIC: BRINGER OF VISION

Pentecost, yet one more of our transliterated words from the Greek, literally means "the fiftieth day"; in the Old Testament, it meant the fiftieth day after the Passover. Associated with notions of harvest and new life in a land of plenty, the Old Testament festival of Pentecost soon gathered to itself the notion of covenant, of a life-giving relationship with God. For Jews, the relationship was embodied in the new Law given to God's people through Moses. For Christians, the day of Pentecost became the day of the Holy Spirit, the celebration of the fulfilling of Jesus' promise of a guide and comforter to his disciples. As Acts tells us, when the day of Pentecost had come, the disciples of Jesus were filled with the Spirit, and were also amazed and perplexed by what had happened to them.

The Bible uses fire, wind, and water as images of the Spirit, the one who in-spires (breathes into) with new insight and possibility. All three are basic elements of life on this planet. Without them we die. All three are elements constantly in motion: the fire flickers, the wind blows, the water flows. All three are also potentially dangerous: the fire burns, and can consume; the wind blows, and can knock down; the water flows, and can drown. To be open to the Spirit, then, is to embrace risk.

Our discussion in Chapter 4 of the prophetic role of the artist must stand as background to these attempts to understand the arts as bringers of vision. The artist is vision-bringer when he or she surprises us out of our ordinary ways and expectations. Vision-bringing is the result of the artist's acceptance of the prophetic role. The prophet breaks open the future partly by reminding us that we must risk confrontation with evil in the present.

If the church throughout the ages has been—or has been supposed to be—a community created by and open to the spirit, it must also be a community schooled to expect the unexpected and to embrace the risks the unexpected brings.

How does—or might—music create small pentecosts for such a community? A reflection on some of the ways the music of Stravinsky opens us to new perceptions of ourselves, our relationships, and reality can show us more clearly how a musician is a bringer of vision.

Stravinsky carried his childhood memories of the rich visual and sonic ceremonial aspects of the Russian Orthodox Church with him throughout his life. Indeed, those memories frequently find their nostalgic expression in his music. Somewhat like Verdi, he held a modestly romanticized view of "church," and it is not always to his religious music that we turn to find his most serious theological statements. This in itself can be seen as an indictment of the failure of even some of the greatest musicians to respond to the theological implications of a church whose "birthday" was the terrifying and overwhelming event described in Acts! It can also, however, be seen as an example of our need to look beyond what we have comfortably defined as religious or sacred or liturgical in order to see the Spirit breaking into the world to recreate and rekindle our vision.

In our brief reflection on Stravinsky as pentecost musician/theologian, the question of evil is the best place to begin. In the midst of the twentieth century, he could not speak "from faith to faith" as Bach or Mozart did, yet, like them, he knew his creative work to be the fruit of his conscience and belief. In 1939, he claimed that "the profound meaning of music and its essential aim . . . is to promote a communion, a union of man with his neighbor and with Being."[1]

Perhaps the clearest, most stereotyped presentation of evil occurs in his earliest music, in *The Firebird*. At the age of twenty-eight, in this 1910 ballet, the composer personified evil as a superhuman power to be conquered only when human power is augmented by revelation from outside the human realm. In the ballet, human beings, enslaved by the Evil One, await redemption from outside themselves. The Evil One's power lies in the secret egg that he carefully protects. The Good One's power lies in the fact that the Firebird has revealed to him the Evil One's secret. In destroying the egg, good overcomes evil permanently. There is innate human sin, the generating egg; there is the savior figure invested with the word, the Good One; there is the dove, the Firebird, descending with "incandescent flame" to reveal new truth. The scene is simple and uncomplicated. Stravinsky's music brilliantly and unambiguously presents the opposing forces.

By 1918, self-exiled in Switzerland during World War I, the composer had come to understand evil with more sophistication, certainly enhanced by his estrangement from his homeland. In *The Story of a Soldier,* the Evil One is no ogre with green claws. He is an exceedingly clever being who pops up in many guises, including a Red Devil parody of himself. He offers the soldier, who is a simple fiddler, delectable choices: power from an old man with a magic book, fortune from a businessman who tells him how to use the book, pleasure from an old hag with pictures of women for hire, prestige from a virtuoso violinist. In short, the Evil One offers him everything. All in exchange for the soldier's fiddle, the one possession that brings him joy. When the soldier makes his choice, his ability to make music disappears.

Now all of this sounds fairly standard. Where is the sophistication, the shift from *The Firebird?* It comes in the conclusion of the work. The Evil One, dressed as the Devil, allows himself to be overcome by the soldier and dragged off. There follows one of the most hilarious moments in music: a "happy ending" punctuated by Stravinsky's wonderful allusion to "A Mighty Fortress Is Our God." Indeed, he suggests, we need not fear the Devil's might. Or need we? To rephrase a line from another familiar hymn, at the sign of triumph, Satan's host doth *not* flee. The final scene shows the unhappy soldier reluctantly returning to his homeland at the urging of his new wife. As soon as he steps over the frontier, there is the unmasked Evil One, no longer needing disguise, the fiddle completely in his control. The soldier cannot resist, and he follows. His final choice was the worst of all: not power or prestige or pleasure, but the past: to turn his back on the future and to exist without hope. Stravinsky supports this bleak ending by having pitch instruments disappear, especially the fiddle sound. At the curtain we hear only primitive drumbeats.

By 1951, Stravinsky had gone farther in his deepening knowledge of good and evil. In *The Rake's Progress,* the Evil One is not seen as an *external* force—neither the ogre of *The Firebird* nor the disguised evil being of *The Story of a Soldier*—but as an *internal* force, part of one's own self. Tom Rakewell's friend and servant, Nick Shadow, shows up at the first instance of potential trouble and functions as Tom's other self. Tom's progress as a rake is delightfully chronicled by the composer. Here the final and crucial choice is not, like that of the soldier, to move into the past. Rather, it is to control the future. Tom, persuaded by Shadow, proclaims himself as God: Creator and not created. Tom sings that "he alone is free who chooses what to will, and wills his choice as destiny."

As a deliberate act of irrational will, Tom marries Baba-the-Turk, a woman with a huge beard. Yet again and again, Tom is temporarily brought to his senses, saved from self-destruction by the memory of his love for Anne, the woman he left behind. Her innocent prayer as she seeks him out, "O God, protect dear Tom," may seem a bit tender under the circumstances, but Stravinsky's music supplies the hope and power that love can bring; he shifts from minor to major thirds and resolves the music to his "dominical" key of C major; no flats, no sharps, a key without guile.

But love, Stravinsky says, is not without limits. Even though Tom Rakewell beats Shadow in a game of cards, winning with the Queen of Hearts, the mark of his self-delusion is indelible. The final scene takes place in a mental ward where Tom, in full fantasy, understands himself as not-himself: as Adonis awaiting his Venus. Anne and her father find him. In a love duet, she and Tom sing of the Here and Now where there is no Absence or Estrangement, no Almost and no Too Late. But it is unreal. And Anne sings gently of that Heavenly City where there is no pain or torment, and she leaves. Love seeks out, finds, comforts—but cannot undo self-deception.

Given his profound understanding of evil, how does Stravinsky see the human response to it? From the end of World

War II until the end of his life, he was more and more concerned with faith worked out in obedience. In the *Mass* of 1948, for instance, the historic symbol of the Christian faith, the Nicene Creed, stands at the center of the sonic architecture, a kind of *A-B-C-B-A* scheme, where the *Kyrie* and *Agnus* are similar in quality (*A*), and the *Gloria* and *Sanctus* a like pair (*B*). It is in that central creed (*C*) that we find Stravinsky relentlessly pounding out three important statements: one holy catholic and apostolic church; one baptism for the remission of sins; resurrection of the dead—past community, present forgiveness, future hope.

In the *Canticum Sacrum* of 1966, he reverses the three virtues, charity, hope, and faith, with faith carrying the music directly to the next section in which Jesus, having exorcised the Evil Spirit from a child, says to the father, "All things are possible to those who believe." The father answers, "I believe; help my unbelief!" (Mark 9:23–24, adapted). Precisely the same series of pitches organizes both movements, binding them together as one.

But it is in the most remarkable of all his music that Stravinsky makes his most profound witness to the relationship of faith, the discernment of good and evil, and God's unexpected word breaking in upon the world. For the struggling state of Israel in 1963, he wrote a terse, intensive musical commentary on the story of Abraham and Isaac. Abraham had faith and obeyed God, even when it meant doing a terrible deed and giving up what he loved most—his only son, Isaac. Through his obedience, Abraham received the blessing of God for himself and for all of his descendants. He is the father of faith for us all, because, as Stravinsky's music makes plain, he heard the new and terrible word, opened himself to it, and found himself filled with grace and a new future.

Hearing the word and doing it; there, says the composer at the age of eighty-one, lies the greatness of the force of nonevil. It is the response of a man of wisdom. It is the response of one who himself has known the Firebird of God. It is like the response of T. S. Eliot:

The dove descending breaks the air
With flame of incandescent terror
Of which the tongue declares
The one discharge from sin and error.
The only hope, or else despair
    Lies in the choice of pyre or pyre—
    To be redeemed from fire by fire.
Who then devised the torment? Love.
Love is the unfamiliar Name
Behind the hands that wove
The intolerable shirt of flame
Which human power cannot remove.
    We only live, only suspire
    Consumed by either fire or fire.[2]

Stravinsky understood and communicated in his music that the choice is made repeatedly in the here and now by each human being. He wrote of himself, "I live neither in the past nor in the future. I am in the present. I cannot know what tomorrow will bring forth. I can only know what the truth is for me today. That is what I am called to serve, and I serve it in all lucidity."[3]

Serving the action of God's Spirit in the present means that churches must be intelligent and intentional about their music. Musically gifted persons need to be identified, encouraged in the discipline of practice, and financially supported so their time may be spent in composing or performing. Musical education must begin early, and weekly lessons add up to considerable cost. In college or conservatory years, the cost, both in money and in time, is immense, not unlike the cost of a medical education. But the cost and the daily hours of practice are investments in the future of the individual, the church, and the wider community.

One of the complexities in our church life is the way in which almost all congregations within a city worship at the same time. Instead of being able to serve two or three groups (Bach was in charge of the music for four congregations in Leipzig; his son supervised six in Hamburg), the church musician serves one, and its budget rarely provides a livelihood.

In many smaller towns, there are frequently a dozen churches competing for the few available musicians, with none able to support the person with a full salary. What might happen were we to listen to this implicit call to unity, to think anew about common baptismal promises, and to open ourselves to new worship schedules and other new ways of providing the music we so earnestly need?

Many churches have begun to provide their own new music. Recently, a parish commissioned a well-known local composer to write music for its service, commemorating a woman of history: Catherine of Sienna. The composer read Catherine's available writings, studied the church's liturgical format, consulted with the clergy and musicians of the parish, then wrote music especially suited not only to the practical requirements of space and time, and to the level of skill of the congregation's performers, but also to the understanding of God that Catherine had acquired and shared. In so doing, the composer imaged for the community new life, new covenant, new relationship.

Many of the same considerations that arise in the hiring of a choreographer also arise when a composer is hired. Contracts are written expressing as precisely as possible what has been agreed upon in preliminary study and conversation. Timetables are made clear, liturgical requirements are shared, resources are listed, and fees are noted. Once such details are in writing, the composer begins to work. Soon something which never was, is. A vision becomes a reality.

Music as bringer of vision helps us understand who we are with new sounds that interpret and give new meaning to our relationships with God and each other. We do not often have a musician of the stature of Stravinsky in our midst, but we do have musicians of considerable skill and insight. We rely on them to make small pentecosts for us through the work they create and the work they choose to perform. If we believe that God speaks to us in the events and people and arts of our lives, we will not be dismayed when those events and people and arts cause us amazement and perplexity. We will know that that is the time, of all times, when we must remain deeply attentive so as not to miss a new pentecost among us!

SUMMARY

Pentecost, new life in the Spirit creating new relationships, is a promise of hope forever renewed. It is the promise
of change, filled with surprise and charged with the unexpected. The human family at different times in its journey
through history has found its way through its ability to recognize and affirm the unpredictable, to ratify the notion that
life is what happens. Not what should or ought to happen, but
what does happen. It is the present tense of being, of becoming, of remembering, that makes the present tension of life
bearable, even creative.

Dance and music speak to us in this same present tense.
Though they can embody tradition so powerfully, their full
power is revealed when they focus the form and content of the
here and now against past community, present struggle and
forgiveness, and future hope.

To live fully in the present is to say yes to the new life of
the Spirit, which moves where and when it will. Who could
have imagined God's way with Moses on the mountain, or
with Abraham and Isaac? Who could have foreseen being called
into action as Isaiah or Abigail or Mary was? Who was prepared for the exodus or the empty tomb? Who has not been
challenged and changed by the great calls to justice of our
time: the peace movement, liberation theologies, the women's
movement? To be open to new life is to have one's imagination
stretched; to be open is also to agree to the hard work of
response.

Musicians and dancers, like all artists, both love and dread
that hard work of response. Their answer to the call of the
Spirit is one of obedience that results in hours of diligent
practice and preparation. That obedience in turn allows them,
from time to time, to be channels of grace to their communities.

Grace means both play and repentance. It means settling
down to live humbly and joyously in the feminine and masculine physicality of our bodies, being willing to live with and
through the sometimes splendid, sometimes terrible story of
all created life. The physical world, the human body, is the

119

only place where life, death, and resurrection happen. It, not the mind estranged or the spirit withdrawn, is the theater of divine revelation. Resurrection assuredly does not follow logically from death. But the body and its death are the only ground there is from which to prepare for resurrection's leap. Through their intense physicality, the arts call us home to that ground. They are a voice from home inviting us to a new covenant with the often baffling physical world, and a new openness to the channels of grace its surprises are.

Robert Yohn and Kristin Peterson in Yohn's Point of Contact. *Photo: Ted Yaple*

Conclusion

The Marriage Feast

To invite artists and their visions into the mainline churches means a commitment to balance the usual verbal and rational approach to faith with the shadow side of human perception and response: the nonverbal and nonanalytic. In the foregoing pages, we have tried to describe and illustrate how the performing arts of music and dance evoke these more intuitive ways of understanding. We have said that the arts foster the capacity for intuitive insight, so that people become more complete unities of body, mind, and spirit, and that the arts can help the church as institution to become more whole in its study, worship, and efforts to bring about justice.

By means of form and discipline, dance and music can offer us visions of the future and images of God's mystery. To say that these arts invite us to be at home in mystery is not in any way to say that they seduce us away from the struggles and commitment of the "real" world. Art is made from and has consequences for the physical and temporal world. Although feeling plays an important part in the creation of art and in our response to it, art is not primarily about or made from feeling—even religious feeling. At its heart, it is a passionate wrestling with form: space, sound, shape, rhythm, line, pitch, texture—until the recalcitrant stuff of the created world blesses artist and audience with a luminous image.

Such images help us to surrender ourselves. We embrace what we perhaps cannot—or at least not yet—rationally affirm.

123

We walk in the company of what we do not logically under-stand. We open doors we never knew were there. When we return to the realm of logic and analysis, we are a little slower to draw mental boundaries separating the impossible from the possible, the silly from the serious, the glorious from the useful.

Unlike classical systematic theology, music and dance do not attempt to convince us of the truth of a complete and rational system of belief. They do not try to explain the uni-verse or our presence in it. Instead, they invite us to come deeper into the landscape of dream, surprise, and longing. What awaits us there is a reunion: a marriage feast celebrating the wedding of intuitive and rational, feminine and masculine, old and new. This celebration goes on in the shifting light and shadow of ambiguous human experience. From its vantage point we see landscapes of sorrow and horror as well as vistas of peace and contentment. At this feast, as at the wedding in Cana, our expectations are turned upside down. What seemed as colorless as water suddenly becomes the richest and headiest of wines.

The process of intuitive knowing to which dance and music invite us is personally transforming; and this transfor-mation, though personal, opens new opportunities to the com-munity. The story of a dance called *Sam Meets His Match* tells something about how and what we can come to know through this process. Through making, performing, and receiving re-sponses to this piece, I have experienced a meeting of dance idea, personal insight, and social issue that sketches part of the shape of the church's relationship to the arts.

I wanted to choreograph a dance about Zacchaeus, the sleazy little tax collector in the Bible whose life is changed by his encounter with Jesus. For many reasons, I put off starting the piece. Meanwhile, I began to meet a terrifying character in my dreams: a young, steel-muscled black man, as full of energy as a coiled spring, wearing black leather and walking a huge Doberman pinscher near railroad tracks at night. He never did anything threatening—just smiled and walked on past. I would wake up in a panic. Finally, I began to realize that, far from being a negative figure, this young man represented a well of energy I hadn't known I had. He was "looking for action" all right, but the action was mine. His presence asked a question: when was I going to recognize and use the raw energy he embodied?

Meanwhile, the Zacchaeus character continued to develop. I was working part-time in San Francisco, and my office window overlooked a Tenderloin street. I sat for hours watching an endless variety of men react to each other and to women; I learned their gestures and postures and movements. Sometime during this period, I saw a picture of my father in a 1940s fedora.

Then I started to choreograph, using three blues guitar pieces by the Rev. Gary Davis. The first one, a version of the United States March, gave me the idea of turning Zack into Sam, a streetwise, still sleazy, tap-dancing version of our own tax-collecting American uncle. This evolution of biblical Zacchaeus into Sam, the national flashman, had something to do with memories from my southern childhood, and also with a need to make the dance's character inescapably contemporary and hard-hitting. The biblical story of Zacchaeus is still the soil from which the dance comes; but the character and his costume, situation, and movement vocabulary are clearly of our own time and place.

As all of this was going forward, I was trying to come to terms with whether and how I, as a woman, could dance this very male character. Why did I want to? Why did the character so clearly have to be a man? Would it—he—work from the audience's point of view? I felt uneasy and somehow embarrassed about *wanting* to dance Sam. I am a woman and should be affirming women by dancing strong female characters! Why did I want and need to bring this slippery, violent man onto the stage? I went on working on the dance while I worried over these questions. But when I put on Sam's costume—white suit and shirt, white jazz shoes and fedora, loud red, white, and blue tie—I had the answer. Sam was no alien, no amusing excursion into party drag. Sam was me. Part of me. I recognized him from the depths of myself, and I loved him. I still love dancing him.

He is anything but a stranger. His outrageous energy and his grin belong to the young black man in my dream. His hat is my father's. His rhythms and cadences come from the alternately soft-voiced and thundering preachers of my childhood. His gestures and his walk are from the Tenderloin sidewalks. Gene Kelly and Bojangles would recognize his jazz-tap footwork. Unmistakably American, unmistakably male, Sam has been a revelation.

Although I started out simply to make a dance, working choreographically and not psychologically, *Sam Meets His Match* represents on one level an unconscious process of meeting and embracing the masculine side of myself. Months after the dance was finished, I realized with a shock that Sam's family tree was even more complex than I had thought. In my last year of seminary, I began having the recurrent dream that I was standing on a street corner next to a headless man wearing a suit and carrying a briefcase. In the dream, I knew that when the traffic light changed, the man would take my head, put it on his shoulders, and walk away down the street. In Sam, I have reclaimed my "stolen property," reintegrating body, mind, and spirit by welcoming this inner sexual opposite.

Other women often relish Sam. Their questions about and responses to him tell me that they, too, recognize him, or at least sense that he has something important to tell them. Some women, after seeing the dance, have sought me out to share their own struggles and relationships with their inner masculine characters. When this kind of response happens, a dance, or any artwork, is functioning as a catalyst for personal integration and reflection. This inner process can go on to inform outer perception and action. What Sam has taught me is that welcoming and learning to know our masculinity if we are female, and our femininity if we are male, is the interior dimension—the intuitive dimension—of creating lasting inclusiveness in the external world.

If we hope to create an inclusive church in a less sexist world, one of our tasks is to acknowledge, to "dance with," these interior opposites. Within the church this is a little-explored area, and one in which the arts may offer the most powerful means of exploration. Of course, the question can and should be raised whether this sort of thing is not better left to Jungian experts and pastoral counselors. The church is not, after all, primarily in the business of therapy. One response to this concern is that counseling is generally for individuals or, at most, couples and families. It is also problem- and crisis-oriented. But the arts, in this area of the integration of masculine and feminine as well as in other areas of intuitive and imagistic perception, offer a gentle, gradual, non-problem solving process to the whole community. They offer the chance for a community, over time, to prepare the internal and external ground for a new vision of things, and to experience together that vision beginning to be true within and among themselves.

The performing arts are particularly good at creating this communal opportunity, because they are usually experienced by a sizable group of people together. In a religious setting, the opportunity for these arts to prepare the ground for a new vision is especially great, because the audience or congregation has probably gathered with a somewhat different agenda than has the usual theater audience. Although enjoyment of what they see and hear is part of their expectation, they are usually present as much because it is a religious event as because it is an art event. Often they have gathered to *do* something together—such as worship—or to pursue some concern together, such as education. This means that a congregation comes to the performing arts in the church expecting to reflect on what they experience, draw meaning from it, and make connections between it and other parts of their lives. Because the audience comes with this expectation, artists and theologians have both the opportunity and the responsibility to encourage people to grapple personally and corporately with what is presented.

A church community present at an art event finds sonic, kinetic, and visual imagery that becomes part of their inner world of thought, feeling, and even dream. (People have very often told me of dreaming about a dance they at first did not "understand," and coming over weeks or months to a new perception of its significance.) A double process founded on this imagery can take place: on the one hand, privately living with these images and noticing the ways they affect one's inner life; on the other, corporately working with the images and responses to them in relation to social and theological concerns. To facilitate this multilevel growing is to nurture *response*-able people who are compassionate unities of body, mind, and spirit.

Ironically, the issue of inclusiveness has been deeply divisive in the church. Feminists and traditionalists oppose each other, with great pain on both sides. No one would suggest the arts as the panacea for this situation; but they can and do offer healing and new opportunities for understanding oneself and the issues involved in the debate. We have most often approached the issue of inclusiveness *as* an issue, in terms of the need for righteousness and justice to redress the historical wrongs against women. But the images and landscapes of artworks offer us an additional approach to understanding the unifying and complex vision of "God created them male and female." This nonrational, non–issue-oriented way invites both women and men to go more deeply into themselves, to walk through the unexpected landscapes there, and to sit down together at the marriage feast of feminine and masculine.

This marriage feast, this momentous occasion, takes place in the volatile border country between dualities. We are as uneasy there as Stravinsky's Isaac on his way up the sacrificial mountain. In *Abraham and Isaac,* Stravinsky's music for Isaac asks over and over, "Why?" Why the sacrifice, why the necessity for creating such confusion and suffering for Abraham, such fear for Isaac? Why is God doing this? What does it mean? Like all human beings, Isaac receives, of course, no real answer. Instead, he and Abraham live out a new image of God's love, made visible by their response to the mysterious—and hair-raising—Word.

When the performing arts of dance and music inform the church's life with their full power, we are all, women and men, enabled to live out more completely the image of God's love as it shapes itself in our own ambiguous experience.

Judith Rock, Cynthia Winton-Henry, and Phil Porter in Rock's Ritual.
Photo: Kingmond Young

Notes

Introduction: Lighting the Shadow Side
1. Anne Wilson Schaef, *When Society Becomes an Addict* (San Francisco: Harper & Row, 1987), p. 64.
2. Emily Dickinson, *Final Harvest: Emily Dickinson's Poems,* ed. Thomas H. Johnson (Boston: Little, Brown, 1960), #311 (764), pp. 189–190.

Chapter One: Dance and Music: Time Arts
1. For a complete discussion of the elements of dance design, see Doris Humphrey's *The Art of Making Dances,* ed. Barbara Pollock (New York: Holt, 1962).
2. Readers interested in the history of dance in the church and the general history of Western dance are referred to many of the dance entries in the Bibliography that follows this Notes section.
3. William Billings, *The Continental Harmony* (Boston: Thomas and Andrews, 1794), p. vii.

Chapter Two: Music, Dance, and Christian Tradition
1. Roger Sessions, *The Musical Experience* (New York: Atheneum, 1967), pp. 18–19.
2. Roger Sessions, *Questions About Music* (Cambridge, Mass.: Harvard University Press, 1970), p. 23.
3. Gregory Thaumaturgous, quoted in Margaret Fisk Taylor, *A Time to Dance* (Philadelphia: United Church Press, 1967), p. 74.
4. G. K. Chesterton, *Orthodoxy* New York: Doubleday, 1959), p. 160.
5. Igor Stravinsky, *The Poetics of Music* (Cambridge, Mass.: Harvard University Press, 1979), pp. 185–187.

Chapter Three: Moses and the Burning Bush
1. Dorothy Sayers, *The Mind of the Maker* (San Francisco: Harper & Row, reprint 1941), pp. 21–22.

2. Paul Hindemith, *A Composer's World* (New York: Doubleday, 1961), p. 70.
3. Hindemith, *A Composer's World,* p. 54.
4. Stravinsky, *The Poetics of Music,* p. 71.
5. John Cage, *Silence* (Middletown, Conn.: Wesleyan University Press, 1961), pp. 76–77.
6. Stravinsky, *The Poetics of Music,* p. 85.
7. Erwin Stein, ed., *Arnold Schoenberg Letters* (New York: St. Martin's Press, 1965), letter 63, 20 April 1923.
8. Stein, *Arnold Schoenberg Letters,* letter 145, 23 September 1932.
9. Arnold Schoenberg's opera *Moses und Aron* (Gertrud Schoenberg, European American Music, 1957), pp. 66–68.
10. Cage, *Silence,* p. 93.

Chapter Four: Performer as Priest and Prophet

1. Romano Guardini, *The Spirit of the Liturgy* (New York: Sheed and Ward, 1940), p. 171.
2. Ibid., p. 173.
3. Peter Shaffer, *Amadeus* (London: Andre Deutsch, 1980), p. 37.
4. Ralph Vaughan Williams, quoted in Donald Jay Grout, *A History of Western Music* (New York: Norton, 1973), p. 672.

Chapter Five: Art as Pentecost

1. Stravinsky, *The Poetics of Music,* p. 25.
2. T. S. Eliot, "Little Gidding," *Four Quartets* (New York: Harcourt Brace Jovanovich, 1971), pp. 37–38.
3. Igor Stravinsky, *An Autobiography* (1936), p. 176.

Bibliography

DANCE

Bachman, E. Louis. *Religious Dances in the Christian Church in Popular Medicine*. London: Allen and Unwin, 1952.

Buechner, Frederick. *Telling the Truth: The Gospel as Tragedy, Comedy, and Fairy Tale*. San Francisco: Harper & Row, 1977.

Capon, Robert Farrar. *Hunting the Divine Fox: Images and Mystery in Christian Faith*. New York: Seabury Press, 1974.

Clark, James M. *The Dance of Death in the Middle Ages and the Renaissance*. Glasgow: Jackson, Son, and Co., 1950.

Cohen, Selma Jean. *The Modern Dance: Seven Statements of Belief*. Middletown, Conn.: Wesleyan University Press, 1966.

De Mille, Agnes. *The Book of the Dance*. London: Paul Hamlyn, 1962.

De Sola, Carla. *The Spirit Moves: A Handbook of Dance and Prayer*. Washington, D.C.: The Liturgical Conference, 1977.

Dietering, Carolyn. *Actions, Gestures, and Bodily Attitudes*. Saratoga, Calif.: Resource Publications, 1980.

Duffy, Natalie Willman. *Modern Dance: An Adult Beginner's Guide*. Englewood Cliffs, N.J.: Prentice-Hall, 1982.

Ellfeldt, Lois. *A Primer for Choreographers*. Palo Alto, Calif.: Mayfield, 1967.

Ellfeldt, Lois, and Carne, Edwin. *Dance Productions Handbook or Later Is Too Late*. Palo Alto, Calif." Mayfield, 1971.

Gagne, Ronald; Kane, Thomas; and VerEcke, Robert. *Introducing Dance in Christian Worship*. Washington, D.C.: Pastoral Press, 1984.

Gardner, John. *On Moral Fiction*. New York: Basic Books, 1978.

Gross, J. B. *The Parson on Dancing*. Brooklyn, N.Y.: Dance Horizons, 1977.

Hanna, Judith Lynne. *To Dance Is Human: A Theory of Nonverbal Communication*. Austin: University of Texas Press, 1979.

Harned, David Bailey. *The Ambiguity of Religion*. Philadelphia: Westminster Press, 1968.

Humphrey, Doris. *The Art of Making Dances*. Edited by Barbara Pollock. New York: Holt, 1962.

Kirstein, Lincoln. *Dance: A Short History of Classical Theatrical Dancing*. Brooklyn, N.Y.: Dance Horizons, 1969.

Mead, G. R. W. *The Sacred Dance in Christendom*. Quest Reprint Series, no. 2. London: John M. Watkins, 1926.

Rock, Judith. *Theology in the Shape of Dance*. Austin, Tex.: The Sharing Co., 1978.

Rock, Judith, and Adams, Doug. *Biblical Criteria in Modern Dance: The Modern Dance as a Prophetic Form*. Austin, Tex.: The Sharing Co., 1980.

Sachs, Curt. *The World History of the Dance*. New York: Norton, 1957.

Sayers, Dorothy L. *The Mind of the Maker*. 1941. Reprint. San Francisco: Harper & Row, 1979.

Shahn, Ben. *The Shape of Content*. Cambridge, Mass.: Harvard University Press, 1957.

Siegel, Marcia B. *The Shapes of Change: Images of American Dance*. Boston: Houghton Mifflin, 1979.

Sorrell, Walter. *The Dance Through the Ages*. New York: Grosset and Dunlap, 1967.

Strong, Roy; Guest, Ivor; and Buckle, Richard. *Designing for the Dancer*. Englewood Cliffs, N.J.: Universe Publishing Co., 1982.

Taylor, Margaret Fisk. *A Time to Dance: Symbolic Movement in Worship*. Revised edition, ed. Doug Adams. North Aurora, Ill.: The Sharing Co., 1976.

Turner, Margery. *New Dance: Approaches to Non-Literal Choreography*. Pittsburgh, Penn.: University of Pittsburgh Press, 1976.

Wigman, Mary. *The Language of Dance*. Translated by Walter Sorrell. Middletown, Conn.: Wesleyan University Press, 1966.

MUSIC

Blume, Friedrich. *Protestant Church Music: A History*. New York: Norton, 1974.

Chase, Gilbert. *America's Music: From the Pilgrims to the Present.* 2d ed. New York: McGraw-Hill, 1966.

Hindemith, Paul. *A Composer's World: Horizons and Limitations.* Garden City, N.Y.: Doubleday, 1961.

Hutchings, Arthur. *Church Music in the Nineteenth Century.* New York: Oxford University Press, 1967.

Le Huray, Peter. *Music and the Reformation in England 1549–1660.* New York: Oxford University Press, 1967.

Mellers, Wilfrid. *Bach and the Dance of God.* London: Faber and Faber, 1980.

————. *Beethoven and the Voice of God.* New York: Oxford University Press, 1983.

————. *Caliban Reborn: Renewal in Twentieth-Century Music.* New York: Harper & Row, 1967.

Routley, Erik. *Church Music and Theology.* Philadelphia: Fortress Press, 1965.

Stravinsky, Igor. *Poetics of Music.* Bilingual ed. Cambridge, Mass.: Harvard University Press, 1970.

Temperley, Nicholas. *The Music of the English Parish Church.* London: Cambridge University Press, 1979.

Acknowledgments

Grateful acknowledgement is made for permission to use the following:

Excerpts from "Erik Satie," copyright © 1958, 1957 by John Cage. Reprinted from Silence by permission of Wesleyan University Press. This piece first appeared in Art New Annual. Excerpt from "Four Statements on the Dance," copyright © 1944 by John Cage. Reprinted from Silence by permission of Wesleyan University Press. This piece first appeared in Dance Observer. Excerpts from "Grace and Clarity," copyright © 1944 by Dance Observer. Reprinted from Silence by permission of Wesleyan University Press. Excerpt from "Little Gidding" in Four Quartets by T. S. Eliot, copyright © 1943 by T. S. Eliot; renewed 1971 by Esme Valerie Eliot. Reprinted by permission of Harcourt Brace Jovanovich, Inc. Excerpt from "Little Gidding" in Four Quartets by T. S. Eliot. Reprinted by permission of Faber and Faber, Ltd. Excerpt from the Musical Experience of Composer, Performer, Listener by Roger Sessions, copyright © 1950 renewed 1978 by Princeton University Press. Excerpt from The Spirit of the Liturgy by Romano Guardini, copyright © 1940. Reprinted by permission of Sheed & Ward. Excerpt from Orthodoxy by G. K. Chesterton, published by Dodd, Mead & Company, Inc. Excerpt from Orthodoxy by G. K. Chesterton, published by A. P. Watt Ltd. Excerpt from Arnold Schoenberg Letters, edited by Erwin Stein, copyright © 1965, St. Martin's Press, Inc., New York. Excerpt from Arnold Schoenberg Letters, edited by Erwin Stein, copyright © 1965, Faber and Faber Ltd., Publishers.

Excerpt from When Society Becomes An Addict by Anne Wilson Schaef, copyright © 1987, Harper & Row, Publishers, Inc. Excerpt from Oxford English Dictionary: The Compact Edition, copyright © 1971, by Oxford University Press. Excerpt from A Time To Dance by Margaret Taylor, copyright © 1967 by United Church Press. Excerpt from Amadeus by Peter Shaffer, copyright © 1981, by Harper & Row, Publishers, Inc. Poem #311 by Emily Dickinson from Final Harvest, edited by T. Johnson. Published by Little, Brown and Company. Excerpt from A History of Western Music by Donald Jay Grout. Published W. W. Norton & Company, Inc. Excerpts from the opera Moses und Aron, © by Gertrud Schoenberg 1957. Copyright

ACKNOWLEDGMENTS

assigned to B. Schott's Soehne. Copyright renewed. All rights reserved. Used by permission of European American Music. Distributors Corporation, Agent for B. Schott's Soehne. Excerpts from the opera Moses und Aron used by permission of Belmont Music Publishers. Copyright 1958 by Gertrud Schoenberg. Copyright renewed 1986 by Belmont Music Publishers. Excerpts from Poetics of Music in the Form of Six Lessons, by Igor Stravinsky, bilingual edition, 1970, reprinted by permission of Harvard University Press. Excerpts from An Autobiography, by Igor Stravinsky, 1936, used by permission of the Stravinsky family.